Trump and Hitler: A Responsible Consideration

By Horace Bloom

This book is a second edition of Donald Trump and Adolf
Hitler: Making a Serious Comparison, published in 2016.

ISBN: 1542586879
ISBN-13: 978-1542586870

Cover image derived from photograph of Donald Trump
by Michael Vadon of Maryland
and photograph of Adolf Hitler by Heinrich Hoffmann.
Both photographs are in the public domain.

DEDICATION

This book is written in acknowledgement of the suffering of the survivors of the Holocaust in Nazi Germany, and to marginalized people in all societies. It is published as a memorial of the decision made on Election Day 2016. It is dedicated to the preservation of the democratic ideals of liberty and equality under the law for all people.

CONTENTS

RESPECT

This book is indebted to the historians who have chronicled the dark days of Nazi Germany and to the journalists of today who continue to detail the plans of those who would undermine our democratic institutions and abuse the power of the government.

INTRODUCTION

American history wasn't supposed to turn this way.

The evening of November 8, 2016 delivered a shock to almost everybody in America. Few people, whether they supported Hillary Clinton or Donald Trump, expected Donald Trump to win the election. Established political polls gave Trump only about a 30 percent chance of defeating Clinton. Rigorously calculated political models showed that, in order to win, Trump would have to take the Electoral College votes of every single one of the states that was within his grasp.

It wasn't likely, but that's exactly what happened.

Clinton supporters began the night in a festive mood, taking photographs of themselves wearing "I voted" stickers and proudly posting them online. Journalists described the outcome as if it had already taken place, and were crafting narratives about the meaning of the first female President.

Not a single major newspaper in the United States had endorsed the candidacy of Donald Trump. His ideas and his behavior were so far outside of the mainstream of responsible political practice that it was inconceivable to political professionals that Trump could receive the support of enough voters to win.

Perhaps the very confidence that Democrats felt in the landslide triumph they thought they had earned made that victory impossible. The biggest factor in Hillary Clinton's loss was that Democratic voters had a remarkably low turnout. Some of that was due to the manipulation of the election in Trump's favor by Russian spies who provoked division within Democratic Party ranks, but more fundamentally, Trump won because almost nobody thought they had to worry about him winning.

Still, even in victory, Donald Trump did not receive a

mandate to enact the agenda he had described as a presidential candidate. Trump lost the popular vote by about three million ballots. In the days before Trump's inauguration, polls showed that trump's favorability rating was only 37 percent. Bill Clinton had a favorability between 60 and 70 percent before his inauguration. Obama's favorability was up in the 80s. Even George W. Bush's support was above 50 percent.

Despite his lack of a mandate, Trump's transition team only increased America's fears about his racist nationalism. Several of the new advisors chosen for the Trump White House had spread communications by white supremacists. The Attorney General nominee Jeff Sessions had made his name by persecuting civil rights workers who were trying to help African-Americans register to vote. When Trump chose Steve Bannon, the man who had made the Breitbart propaganda site into a voice for American Nazis, to be his top political advisor, white supremacists across America cheered.

Trump supporters responded to the signals. Spray-painted swastikas appeared across America, as students in high schools, middle schools and elementary schools began sharing Nazi salutes and shouting "Sieg heil"!

Hispanics began to be harassed by groups of Trump supporters shouting, "Build that wall!" African-Americans were physically assaulted and told to "go back to Africa". Girls were groped in public by boys acting out of the new confidence that no one would stop them, given that Donald Trump had just been elected President after bragging about his sexual assault of women.

In many places, Donald Trump's nationalist slogan Make America Great Again was shifted to become "Make America White Again." In Massachusetts, residents of one neighborhood woke up to messages reading, "Gas the Jews" mixed in with "Trump 2016".

In Washington DC, members of a group with the deceptively mild title of National Policy Institute met in a federal building for a convention discussing how white nationalism in America would benefit from the leadership of Donald Trump. The organization didn't try to hide its Nazi identity as its leader, Richard Spencer, shouted out the equivalent of "Heil Hitler" for our own time, calling, "Hail Trump, hail our people, hail victory!" His followers knew how to respond, shouting "Sieg heil," while raising their arms in stiff Nazi salutes.

Although many Republican voters had reassured themselves that Trump would surely become more presidential after his victory, and work to bring Americans together, the Trump transition only became more divisive. Trump holed himself up in his Manhattan penthouse, shutting down traffic on 5th Avenue day after day, while sending out messages on Twitter that were even more erratic and unhinged than those seen before Election Day, with strange rants against his "enemies".

Unlike most presidents-elect, who hunker down and begin the hard work of preparing for the difficult job ahead of them, Trump sought out new opportunities to provoke and disturb. He blasted comedians, demanded apologies from Broadway shows, and called Hollywood actors flunkies. Turning his sights to China, Trump provoked international incidents that by Inauguration Day had led to warnings from Beijing that war could be imminent.

Trump's most extreme promises did not fade away. He insisted that the wall would be built, that Muslims would be forced to sign up in national religious registries, and that deportation squads would be formed on day one to round up millions of people in the United States and drag them into exile through the use of force.

This unpresidential behavior became even more erratic when news broke that spy agencies working directly under orders from Vladimir Put had in worked throughout 2016 to infiltrate state and local boards of elections in the United States, gather and weaponized information to damage Hillary Clinton's campaign, all working with the explicit purpose of ensuring that Donald Trump would become the next President of the United States. Once again, Trump's slogan shifted, but this time from Make America Great Again to Make Russia Great Again.

The scandal expanded into a new stage as a British intelligence report that had been circulating among journalists and politicians leaked out into the open, alleging that Trump had been recruited as an intelligence asset by Russian agents who set him up in honey traps, videotaping Trump in unorthodox sexual acts with Russian prostitutes. As intelligence officials warned that Trump could be controlled through blackmail by Moscow, Americans began laughing at a dizzying array of jokes about what came to be called GoldenShowersGate.

Massive crowds of protesters in the nation's capitol threatened to overwhelm the inauguration itself, as Americans prepared signs of resistance to the man they called Adolf Trump, the Orange Fuhrer. These were clear references to Adolf Hitler, expressing the fear many Americans felt about Trump's authoritarian tendencies, his racism, his megalomaniacal personality.

Did Americans just elect a Nazi to be President of the United States? Could Donald Trump be the Adolf Hitler of our time? Are people's fears about the new administration justified?

What's obvious to everyone is that Donald Trump won't follow any standard model for what the President of the United States should be. Where some people perceive a monster, others see a fool over his hear, while others find a trickster who merely wears the disguise of a totalitarian bully to outmaneuver his opponents.

Trump has made it the defining feature of his political identity to break the rules that have traditionally restrained America's leaders. His followers thrill to see his defiance of convention. It makes them feel vicariously empowered to witness his rebellion. However, a person who feels free to ignore the rules that restrain other people may also feel free to ignore the rules that keep other people safe.

As the most unpredictable politician in American history crosses the threshold into the most powerful office in the world, it has become even more important to consider the questions that provoked the first edition of this book. That was back in March of 2016. In just a little under one year, a great deal has changed. Nobody really knows what might happen next.

Back then, the Republican primaries were moving solidly in Donald Trump's favor, but the conventional wisdom was that Trump could not possibly become the nominee. Surely, people thought, the Republican establishment would put its support behind a more responsible candidate, and Trump would become just a strange blip in American political history. The idea that he could actually sit as President was too bizarre for many people to take seriously.

Just so, in January of 2017, many Americans still can't take Trump seriously. His opponents still laugh at his blunders and blustering. However, the President of the United States is not a clown. As President of the United States, Donald Trump has nuclear weapons at his disposal. Whatever Trump does with his new power, the consequences will be no joke.

So, this second edition, revised to include much of the relevant history of Trump's rise to power since early 2016, takes its subject seriously. This isn't a book that simply observes that Donald Trump and Adolf Hitler have a striking number of similarities, as a form of insult to the 45th President. Instead, this book aims to understand Trump by examining both similarities and differences.

Precisely because Trump is so unpredictable, Americans need a solid frame of reference through which to consider just what kind of leader he really is. Hitler provides a useful frame of reference, because almost everybody agrees, regardless of differences in political opinion, that Hitler would be the worst president imaginable.

There are many arguments that have been made against comparing Trump and Hitler, and most of those arguments rely upon the strawman fallacy. No, of course Trump is not literally Hitler. Of course Trump has not done all the terrible things that Hitler did while he ruled Germany. He couldn't possibly have done those things, even if he wanted to – he just now stepped into the Oval Office. Even Hitler took many years to achieve his full, terrible potential.

As President, Trump is not going to precisely replicate Hitler's record. This is the 21st century, and the United States is not Germany. Whatever is going to happen under Trump, it's going to be different than anything the world has ever seen before.

However, it is irresponsible for us to simply take the attitude of waiting and seeing what's happening, while suspending our judgment. Hoping for the best is not what citizenship in a democracy is all about. Elections are just one way for people to participate in democratic government.

Whatever action American citizens choose to take in response to the inauguration of Donald Trump as President, those actions should have a basis in solid information. After an election in which fake news, foreign propaganda, and outright ignorance seemed to be the dominant influence, the best response begins with education.

Trump gained the presidency by throwing the American political system into disorder. It's time for Americans to confront that disorder by examining its content. While Trump is unique, his tactics and beliefs are not completely without precedent. We ignore the parallels between Trump and Hitler at our peril.

INTRODUCTION TO THE FIRST EDITION

How dare you compare Donald Trump to Adolf Hitler!

The reaction of many people to comparisons of Donald Trump and Adolf Hitler is a simple rejection of the right to make such a comparison. To even contemplate the idea that any contemporary political leader could have some similarities to Adolf Hitler has become a cultural taboo.

When the editorial board of the Fresno State Collegian wrote that, "Trump represents the rise of a new Hitler and is capable of the same atrocities. It's like we're in the 1930s on a runaway train barreling toward World War III," readers expressed outrage, not at Trump's policies, but at the declaration that Trump and Hitler could be compared.

"I can't believe they published that! Disgraceful at best," one reader complained. "The old internet rule is that the first person in an argument to compare their opponent to Hitler automatically loses," advised another.

The taboo is a source of great temptation, however. History teacher Tom Richey paid deference to the taboo, telling his students that, "I don't want to dignify that stuff," and declaring it absurd to even to think of comparing the American Confederacy with Nazi Germany. Still, Richey couldn't help himself. In spite of his warning to his students, he went ahead and posted a satirical video to YouTube, making superficial comparisons between Adolf Hitler and Donald Trump, pointing out, for instance, that while Hitler had a goofy mustache, Trump has goofy hair on top of his head.

These kinds of superficial, glancing assessments make it easy to dismiss comparisons between Donald Trump and Adolf Hitler as absurd and unhinged. Sometimes, they certainly are. Is it, however, inherently ridiculous to make such comparisons?

There are, to put it broadly, two common reactions to the atrocities that were committed by Adolf Hitler and Nazi Germany. The first is that they must never be forgotten, that we need to keep the lessons of the Third Reich fresh in people's minds, in order to make sure that nothing like them can ever happen again.

The second reaction is to conclude that references to Adolf Hitler and the Nazi Party should be severely restricted to literal retellings of history and simple, direct condemnations. People who adhere to this line of thinking seek to place the memory of Nazi Germany into a kind of time capsule, separated from the rest of human history. In particular, they insist, current events must never be considered in the light of Nazi history, and no one should ever compare any living person to Hitler.

Justifications for the strict conceptual isolation of Nazi Germany from people who are comparable Nazis in all subsequent history include the assertion that to compare any current event to the activities of the Nazis minimizes the particular historical reality experienced by those who suffered under Hitler's rule.

For example, when James Crotty, the author of the book How To Talk American, asserts that "comparing Trump to Hitler is the worst kind of hate speech," writing that, "I find it deeply insulting to all those who died in the Holocaust to have their sacrifice cheaply denigrated in this way. When we apply a Nazi comparison to someone or something that does not fit that comparison, then Nazism and the Holocaust lose their power to shock us. And they must never lose that power. If they do, which is quickly happening right now, when something diabolical does come along again in this world, we have no way to identify it, let alone stop it, because we've cried Nazi wolf so often that the comparison has lost its power to persuade."

There is a rather circular nature to Crotty's argument. He asserts that comparing present day politicians to Hitler is "hate speech" because it makes the idea of Adolf Hitler seem too familiar, so that, when politicians come along who are like Adolf Hitler, we won't be able to meaningfully make the comparison. What Crotty fails to account for is the possibility that Donald Trump might actually have some similarities to Adolf Hitler that are worth noting.

Crotty, like other advocates of the avoidance strategy, cites something called "Godwin's Law". Unlike an actual law, the identity of Godwin's Law has a rather fluid nature, often being redefined to suit the purposes of those who use it. It began, however, as a specific idea, composed in 1990, in the form of an immutable law of physics, by Mike Godwin, a lawyer who had grown exasperated with fast any easy comparisons of practically any disliked political idea or leader to Hitler and his Nazi ideology. "As an online discussion grows longer, the probability of a comparison involving Nazis or Hitler approaches 1," Godwin wrote.

Other incarnations of Godwin's Law state things such as "If you mention Adolf Hitler or Nazis within a discussion thread, you've automatically ended whatever discussion you were taking part in," or, more simply, "Invoke the Nazis and you've lost the argument."

People who disapprove of comparisons of present-day politicians to Adolf Hitler tend to refer to Godwin's Law as if it were an actual law, or at least a cultural principle that is generally understood and accepted. However, there's never been any general cultural consensus around Godwin's Law, much less any formal establishment of the idea as an enforceable code. The premise that people who bring up comparisons of current political ideologies to the Nazis automatically lose an argument has never been agreed upon or substantiated with any empirical research.

Responding to these efforts at censorship, journalist Glenn Greenwald writes, "The very notion that a major 20th Century event like German aggression is off-limits in political discussions is both arbitrary and anti-intellectual in the extreme. There simply are instances where such comparisons uniquely illuminate important truths." Greenwald argues that the principles derived from the Nuremberg Trials were intended to be applied in the future, not "shrouded with a code of silence."

Recently, Mike Godwin himself has spoken out against the way that Godwin's Law is being used to try to stop comparisons of Donald Trump to Adolf Hitler. "If you're thoughtful about it and show some real awareness of history, go ahead and refer to Hitler or Nazis when you talk about Trump. Or any other politician," he wrote.

Godwin advised his fans that "The best way to prevent future holocausts, I believe, is not to forbear from Holocaust comparisons; instead, it's to make sure that those comparisons are meaningful and substantive."

Despite Godwin's own protestations, Godwin's Law has begun to be used as a form of censorship by followers of Trump, a tool for shutting down well-informed critiques of the candidate's policies and techniques. They're using Godwin's Law as an article of faith, and canonizing Holocaust survivors as martyrs in their efforts to stifle consideration of the broad political movement that Trump has harnessed.

The truth is that Holocaust survivors are not merely characters from the past. They're getting older, but many of them are still around.

It would be a mistake to suggest that all Holocaust survivors share the same opinions about current events in general, or Donald Trump in particular. However, it is worth noting that many survivors have spoken out about the similarities they perceive between Donald Trump and Adolf Hitler.

Eva Schloss, a former prisoner at the Auschwitz Nazi concentration camp and a sister-in-law to Anne Frank, has stated, "If Donald Trump becomes the next president of the U.S. it would be a complete disaster. I think he is acting like another Hitler by inciting racism. During his U.S. presidential campaign he has suggested the "total and complete shutdown of Muslims entering the United States," as well as pledging to build a wall between the U.S. and Mexico to keep illegal immigrants out."

Another Auschwitz survivor, Irene Weiss, explains that her concern is not about whether comparisons between Trump and Hitler are appropriate. Her concern is about the demagoguery exhibited by Donald Trump and his competitors in the 2016 presidential race. "I am exceptionally concerned about demagogues," she says. "They touch me in a place that I remember. I know their influence and, unfortunately, I know how receptive audiences are to demagogues and what it leads to."

Al Munzer, who was hidden from the Nazis as a baby, worries about Donald Trump's "message of hate," and offers a direct rebuttal to those who seek to shut down discussions of how Hitler's ideology may be manifesting itself in the campaigns of today's political leaders: "Thinking that Germany was somehow unique is wrong."

The people who fought Adolf Hitler and his armies in

World War II are not honored by efforts to suppress discussions of equivalents of Hitler's actions and Nazi ideology in our own time. Greenwald points out that those who prosecuted Nazis for their war crimes after World War II did so in the hopes that people in the future would remember the Nazi atrocities, and use them as a point of comparison to maintain standards of human rights. "A primary point of the Nuremberg Trials was to seize on the extraordinary horror of what the Germans did in order to set forth general principles to be applied not only to the individual war criminals before the tribunal, but more important, to all countries in the future," he writes.

Historian Laurence Rees warned his readers that, "The desire to be led by a strong personality in a crisis, the craving for our existence to have some kind of purpose, the quasi worship of 'heroes' and 'celebrities,' the longing for salvation and redemption: none of this has changed in the world since the death of Hitler in April 1945."

The precise historical factors that allowed Adolf Hitler to establish Nazi Party to control over Germany will never be repeated. The more general cultural and social factors that led to the founding of the Third Reich, however, may well reoccur many times in the future, leading to terrifying regimes that resemble the Nazi regime in its most dreadful respects, although differing in many of the particularities of their manifestations.

There is a difference between comparing someone with Hitler and equating them with Hitler. Saying that someone is "just like Hitler" is both rhetorically extreme and factually wrong. Hitler was a unique figure in a distinct historical context. No one will ever be just like him. But someone can be enough like him that comparisons reveal significant things, and the similarities between Hitler and Donald Trump are significant enough to cause genuine concern.

Practically speaking, the horse is out of the barn. People from all kinds of backgrounds, from all around the world, are already talking about the similarities and differences between Adolf Hitler and Donald Trump. There's no centralized effort to try to manufacture these discussions. Rather, the topic is spontaneously emerging in conversations because there's something about Trump that reminds people of Hitler.

Trump himself has been confronted on the issue. George Stephanopoulos of ABC News said to Trump, "You're increasingly being compared to Hitler. Does that give you any pause at all?"

When Trump responded, he at first seemed to distance himself from the Nazi leader's ideology, but then embraced another racist atrocity of World War II – the imprisonment of American citizens of Japanese ancestry by President Franklin Roosevelt. "No," Trump responded. The comparison between himself and Hitler didn't give him pause, "because what I'm doing is not different than what FDR, FDR's solution for Germans, Italians, Japanese, many years ago... Take a look at presidential proclamations 2525, 2526, and 2527 having to do with alien Germans, alien Italians, alien Japanese, and what they did. You know, they stripped them of their naturalization proceedings. They went through a whole list of things. They couldn't go five miles from their homes. They wouldn't let them use radios, flashlights, I mean, take a look at what FDR did many years ago... I don't like doing it at all. It's a temporary measure, until representatives, many of whom are grossly incompetent, until our representatives can figure out what's going on."

In this moment, we encounter the complexity that arises when people attempt to compare a present-day political leader with Adolf Hitler. Even in denying his similarity to Hitler, Trump proposed using a discredited, racist tactic of forcing large numbers of Americans into concentration camps, as was done to Japanese-Americans during World War II.

The Americans were the enemies of Nazi Germany, of

course, but the internment was like an echo of Nazi ideology here in the United States. President Roosevelt was acting something like Adolf Hitler when he signed the order to round up Japanese-Americans and treat them like criminals. So, in a literal way, Trump's response to Stephanopoulos is a rejection of his similarity to Hitler, while on a deeper level, Trump's response confirmed many Americans' concern that Trump would impose a racist, nationalist, authoritarian ideology similar to that of the Nazis if he were elected President.

This interaction shows why a serious consideration of the comparison of Donald Trump and Adolf Hitler is necessary. We won't come to an adequate understanding of this apparent historical echo through quick television interviews, short online articles, YouTube videos, and pugnacious candidate debates. Through such resources, we are exposed to a small piece of a much larger, more complex cultural dynamic.

American voters, and the concerned citizens of the world, are struggling to form a broader and deeper understanding of Donald Trump, to understand how to react to him. We have never seen an American presidential candidate like him before. It is the goal of this book to help provide, through the context of the darkest chapter of the last hundred years, a different kind of insight into the kind of leader that Trump might become, if we allow him to rise to power.

CHAPTER 2:
THE BIOGRAPHIES OF
TRUMP AND HITLER

"Many people have stated that Adolf Hitler was evil, mad, or crazy. The really scary thing is that Hitler was a man." – Jennifer Rosenberg

Photograph by Heinrich Hoffmann, in the public domain

The strange thing about Adolf Hitler is that he was at the simultaneously terrifyingly powerful and ridiculous. For an epitome of pure evil, he was extremely easy to snicker at, from a distance.

One of the most common rebuttals to Trump-Hitler comparisons is to state that, while Adolf Hitler killed millions of people, Donald Trump only says mean things about people. Obviously, according to this line of reasoning, there can be no comparison between the two.

Such dismissals miss an essential point, however: Adolf Hitler did not kill millions of people before he became Chancellor of Germany. Hitler became the killer of millions only after he gained control over the government. His reign of terror could not begin until he reigned.

The comparison of Adolf Hitler at the height of Nazi brutality in Germany with Donald Trump at the very moment that he has become President of the United States is indeed absurd. The apt comparison is between Donald Trump as he steps into the White House and Adolf Hitler at the instant that he had gained political office, but not yet used it. When a comparison is made within this framework, important distinctions between the two politicians remain, but the idea of assessing the similarities between them no longer seems quite so ridiculous.

The essential question that this book confronts is not whether Donald Trump is at present a brutal dictator who has imposed a harsh totalitarian regime over his own nation and unleashed a terrible war against nations around the world. The essential question for Americans at this moment is whether Donald Trump could become a dictator of this sort. The matter under consideration is whether, in electing Donald Trump as President of the United States, the American people have made a mistake similar to that which was made by the Germans who allowed Adolf Hitler to become Chancellor of their nation.

It may seem silly to suppose that Donald Trump could ever make himself anything like a dictator over the USA.

However, the apparently ludicrous nature of this scenario is actually one of the most fundamental similarities between the political ascent of Adolf Hitler and the political ascent of Donald Trump.

In his account of the rise and fall of Adolf Hitler, Laurence Rees observed, "In 1913, when Adolf Hitler was twenty-four years old, nothing about his life marked him out as a future charismatic leader." To most people outside Germany, Hitler seemed like nothing more than a cruel clown until he attained the position of Chancellor.

Photograph by Heinrich Hoffmann, in the public domain

Adolf Hitler was easy to dismiss precisely because he was outlandish in both his mannerisms and his ideas. The same cartoonish demeanor led many Americans to presume in June 2015 that Donald Trump's presidential candidacy was nothing more than a joke, or a casual bit of self-indulgence that would quickly flame out. Only in hindsight can we see that the Trump for President campaign was never anything of the sort.

Let us now put aside the facile dismissals of the Trump-Hitler comparison, and make a serious consideration of the matter. This chapter begins by examining the biographies of the two leaders.

A biographical comparison of Adolf Hitler and Donald Trump needs to begin with an some debunking of some false claims about supposedly direct links between Donald Trump and Adolf Hitler. In December 2015, a satirical web site published an article declaring that Donald Trump is closely related to Adolf Hitler – that Trump's paternal grandmother was married to Hitler's grand uncle, Johann Schicklgruber.

This story is completely fictional. It was made up as a joke, and unfortunately, some people have been too dense to see it for that.

Even if the story were true, it would be irrelevant. It might be interesting if Adolf Hitler were revealed to be Donald Trump's secret grandfather, but the idea that there could be some taint for Trump that comes from being a distant cousin of Hitler is ridiculous. Raving nationalism is not known to be a genetic trait that can be passed down from generation to generation through simple biological ancestry.

It is true that Donald Trump has a significant amount of German heritage, but that's true of the majority of Americans. People with German ancestry are the largest ethnic group in the United States.

In the interest of disclosure, I'll share the fact with you that one of my own family, an uncle on my mother's side, was a general in the Nazi military during World War II. That doesn't make me a Nazi. Here I am, despite this connection to Hitler's army, writing a book with the fundamental principle that the Third Reich was a terrible stain on world history.

As a person of German ancestry, Donald Trump does share one interesting piece of history with Hitler – the transformation of his family name. In the case of the Nazi Fuhrer, the change was from Hiedler to Hitler. In the case of the billionaire Republican presidential candidate, the change was to Trump from Drumpf.

One wonders if Donald Trump might have grown up with a smaller tendency toward self-aggrandizement if his last name had sounded more like a tired sigh instead of representing a special ability to transcend ordinary limits in a game of cards. We will, of course, never know if this would have been the case.

A second false claim linking Donald Trump to the Nazi Party has been built upon a conspiracy theory spread by a large number of right wing media organizations, including Fox News and Investor's Business Daily. You see a representation of it in this graphic, which has been widely distributed through social media:

The charge that Donald Trump and Barack Obama are being controlled by George Soros is quite serious. As such, it requires substantial proof. If people are going to accuse Donald Trump of secretly being controlled by George Soros, who is then alleged to be a "former Nazi sympathizer", then they had better be able to come up with concrete evidence that their allegations are true.

Conspiracy theories about a New World Order, although they are sometimes posed in terms of opposition to Nazi ideology, as in the example above, actually advance a central tenet of Nazi ideology: The belief that wealthy Jews secretly control the entire world. Although the conspiracy theory claims to be shocked that George Soros would collaborate with the Nazis, it is itself a propaganda tool of those promoting an antisemitic distortion that the Nazis would have admired.

For confirmation of this interpretation, we can go directly to the primary center of NeoNazi activity online – the Stormfront web site. "Lrapsody", a sustaining member of Stormfront, repeats the Trump-Soros-Nazi conspiracy, but from a different angle, writing that, "Trump owes a lot of money to Jew George Soros and other wall street Jews. He is completely disingenuous. Seems the Jews have fooled a few with their new star puppet."

In this version of the conspiracy theory alleging that Soros controls Donald Trump, Soros is given the role of representing "the Jews", and not the Nazis at all. The conspiracy theory is so dominated by its own hate that it twists itself into garbled chains of flawed logic that lead nowhere but deep into incoherence.

If Barack Obama and Donald Trump were actually controlled by a single puppet master, they would support the same policies, but on most issues, Obama and Trump are on opposite sides. Obama is pro-choice, Trump is pro-life. Obama is pro-regulation, Trump is anti-regulation. Obama is for fighting climate change, Trump refuses to acknowledge even that climate change exists. You get the picture.

Finally, all existing evidence about the political preferences of George Soros in the 2016 presidential election points to the conclusion that Soros is a determined opponent of Donald Trump, rather than his puppet master. In December 2015, Soros expressed his opposition to the election of Donald Trump in an editorial published in The Guardian, writing that "as 2016 gets underway, we must reaffirm our commitment to the principles of open society and resist the siren song of the likes of Donald Trump and Ted Cruz, however hard that may be."

Aside from this conspiracy theory's lack of structural integrity, its most alarming premise is not supported by the evidence that's available to us. The single information source used by people repeating the story contradicts the allegations of Nazi collaboration. What's more, the testimony of witnesses who observed George Soros during World War II shows that he was a fugitive from the Nazis, rather than their partner in the Holocaust.

It is alleged by proponents of the New World Order conspiracy theory that George Soros chose to go around Budapest, posing as a Christian, while helping Nazis to loot the homes of wealthy Jewish families that were forced to flee. This allegation is entirely based upon an interview of George Soros conducted on the CBS TV show 60 Minutes by Steve Kroft back in 1998.

In this interview, Kroft kept questioning Soros about whether he felt any sense of guilt for having gone out with a representative of the Nazis in Hungary, and, in the words of Kroft, "helped in the confiscation of property from the Jews".

Soros stammered, and responded that, "Well, of course I could be on the other side or I could be the one from whom the thing is being taken away. But there was no sense that I shouldn't be there, because that was, well, actually, in a funny way, it's just like in markets, that if I weren't there, of course, I wasn't doing it, but somebody else would, would, would be taking it away anyhow. And it was the -- whether I was there or not, I was only a spectator, the property was being taken away. So the, I had no role in taking away that property. So I had no sense of guilt."

This sounds pretty damning. It sounds as if, during World War II, George Soros took on a job in which he worked with the Nazis to steal from Jewish families that were being shipped off to concentration camps. It's sounds downright evil.

Things begin to sound quite different when more of the truth about what George Soros did under the Nazi occupation of Hungary is revealed.

For one thing, at the time of the episode that 60 Minutes questioned Soros about, he was just a 14 year-old boy.

For another thing, Soros wasn't in the habit of going out to the homes of "the Jews" and stealing their property in the name of the Nazi regime. He went out to a Jewish home, the extensive estate of a wealthy Jewish family, the Kornfelds, that had fled the country.

Also, Soros didn't actually help loot the home. He walked around the estate, talked to staff members, rode a horse, and then left.

Finally, there's the reason that Soros traveled to that home: Soros had been separated from his family. When the Nazis invaded Hungary, Soros had been left at the home of an Christian employee of the Hungarian Agricultural Ministry with the name of Baumbach. His father paid Baumbach to pretend that Soros was his son. Young Soros didn't choose to go to the Kornfeld home on his own, but was taken there by Baumbach.

In order to survive, George Soros had to pretend that he was a Christian, and that his name was Sandor Kiss. Baumbach was given the odious task of looting homes of Jewish families, and had Soros accompany him to the Kornfeld estate, because the trip would take Baumbach three days. Baumbach was afraid that if he left Soros alone back at his house, he might be discovered, seized, and taken off to a concentration camp.

So, the conspiracy theory that supposes that Donald Trump is being secretly controlled by a Nazi collaborator, who in turn is working for a Jewish New World Order cabal, is completely bogus. Soros wasn't a Nazi collaborator, but a fugitive from the Nazis. The Jewish New World Order is itself a neoNazi fantasy.

It's telling that the conspiracy theory about a Nazi plot to control Trump through George Soros quickly faded away once the Republican primary contest was over. It wasn't used against Trump during the general election at all. That's because he strange story was an artifact of a squabble between competing factions of white supremacists who favored different Republican presidential candidates. By the time of the Republican National Convention, American white supremacists were solidly united behind Trump

Ridiculous conspiracy theories such as this should remind us that, it is easy to slip into wild, irresponsible conjecture while making comparisons between Donald Trump and Adolf Hitler. Wild conjecture can be fun, but it is not the purpose of this book. The stakes are too high to play fast and loose. If the comparisons between Trump and Hitler are to have any value, it will be essential to stick to the facts, without distortion.

To engage in a serious comparison of the biographies of Donald Trump and Adolf Hitler, it is essential to acknowledge some remarkable differences between the two men. These differences begin with their status at birth.

Adolf Hitler was born poor. His father worked hard to financially-struggling, socially obscure family with a history of peasant labor.

William Shirer, a journalist who lived in Germany through the rise of the Nazi power into the Third Reich, explains that Hitler was born into a family with little money to spare, and descended into even greater poverty when he moved to Vienna as a young man. "He lived in flophouses or in the almost equally miserable quarters of the men's hostel," Shirer writes, "staving off hunger by frequenting the charity soup kitchens of the city."

Whatever we think of what he made of himself, no one can deny that Hitler was a true self-made man. He rose to absolute authority from absolute obscurity, sometimes even sleeping outside on park benches in a threadbare coat because he had nowhere else to go.

People often poke fun at Hitler's initial career as an artist, and it's true that he wasn't very successful. He was denied admittance into art school, and his paintings never sold for much money. Most of them were sold merely as place fillers to merchants who found that they could sell picture frames more readily when if there was already a painting within them.

This much must be said for Hitler's career as an artist: He was able to keep himself alive with his painting work. He started the business nearly from nothing. The only financial support he ever received for this venture from his family was a tiny bit of money from his aunt – enough to buy some paint and brushes.

Though he considered himself German, the future Fuhrer wasn't even born in Germany. He was born on the border of Bavaria and Austria, in the minor town of Braunau am Inn. His later Anschluss of Austria into Germany has widely been interpreted as a consequence of his childhood in these borderlands, looking into Germany from the outside.

It's difficult to imagine how the birth of Donald Trump could be more different from Hitler's. Unlike his main Republican opponent, Ted Cruz, he was born squarely inside the borders of the United States, to a family living in New York City.

Donald Trump was born rich. His father, Fred Trump, made a fortune as a real estate developer, and provided his son with an easy path into a lucrative business.

By the time that Donald Trump graduated from college, he was already a millionaire. Even as a student at the Wharton School of Business, Trump was able to make a healthy amount of money through a business project at an apartment complex that had been bought by his father for 5.7 million dollars. Adolf Hitler could have never dreamed of receiving such a huge investment in his early career.

When Trump graduated from school, he didn't have to struggle to find work. His father gave him a good-paying job with excellent opportunities for advancement.

Despite these extreme economic advantages, Trump claims that his story is one of overcoming hardship. "My whole life really has been a 'no' and I fought through it," Trump told a crowd of his supporters recently. "It has not been easy for me. It has not been easy for me, and you know I started off in Brooklyn. My father gave me a small loan of a million dollars."

Though he enjoyed some luxury later in life, to young Adolf Hitler, a loan of a million dollars would have felt in no way "small". In that way, Hitler was more like most Americans today, who can expect no more assistance from their parents upon graduation than a few thousand dollars.

Even if Hitler's father had been more financially successful, it is doubtful that he would have granted his son a million dollar loan. Unlike Trump, who idolized his father, Hitler detested his father, who had beaten him regularly from a young age.

Hitler was determined to get away from his father as soon as possible, not just to escape the physical blows, but evade being sucked into his father's uninspiring professional status. The elder Hitler was proud of his job as a civil servant, but young Adolf regarded such a career as a prison. He dreamed of being a "master of my own time." Writing his manifesto and memoir Mein Kampf, Hitler recalled, "I did not want to become a civil servant, no, and again no. All attempts on my father's part to inspire me with love or pleasure in this profession by stories from his own life accomplished the exact opposite."

Hitler's defiance of his father's authority was mirrored by his opposition to the authority of the adults at school. His teachers soon came to regard him as "argumentative, autocratic, self-opinionated and bad-tempered, and unable to submit to school discipline."

Trump shared Hitler's tendency toward behavioral problems in school, but these difficulties led to vastly different consequences, because Trump had a wealthy father. Fred Trump was on the board of trustees of the private school that his son attended, and so held some influence over matters of discipline when the adolescent Donald got into trouble.

Eventually, when his son's behavior became too disturbing to sweep under the rug any longer, Fred Trump sent Donald to a private military boarding school, the New York Military Academy, 60 miles up the Hudson River from Manhattan.

The Hitler family didn't have enough money to send their son to a private boarding school, so Adolf could only remain in a school where his studies would be directed to learning the skills necessary to establish him in a mediocre post as a civil servant. There was to be no training in the skills he would need to become the artist he aspired to be.

Hitler was stuck, and so, he engaged in the only form of protest available to him. He refused to study for his classes, hoping that his father would break down and allow him to finally train as a painter.

There was, alas, no compromise. So, although Hitler had consistently good grades before the conflict with his father, they degraded to the state of nearly complete failure. Hitler dropped out before he could graduate, drifting for a few years after his father's early death before finally leaving for Vienna. For the rest of his life, Hitler despised academics.

In contrast, once young Trump arrived at the elite military academy, he seemed to accept the will of his father, whom he became determined to emulate. Trump graduated at the top of his class. Whatever his social advantages, here is no denying that Trump possesses a sharp mind.

Whereas Hitler drifted through a series of short-lived jobs before building up his small living as a painter, Trump remained in school, attending Fordham University before transferring to the Wharton School of Business to gain a degree in real estate. Unlike Hitler, Trump was perfectly happy to pursue a degree designed to gain him admittance to his father's line of work.

Although Trump was an able student in his younger days, as an adult he has drifted into the same anti-intellectual attitude adopted by Hitler. Urging his voters to turn out to participate in a Republican caucus, Trump distanced himself from the political sophistication of GOP insiders, telling his audience that, "I'm not going to use the word 'caucus'. I'm just going to use just 'vote'. What the hell is caucus? Nobody even knows what that means."

Of course, plenty of people understand what caucuses are, and how they work. That isn't the point. Trump derives pleasure, as Hitler did, in mocking the learning of others.

Not long after their schooling was done, both Hitler and Trump faced a gut-wrenching decision: Whether to fight for their countries on the battlefield. When World War I came, Adolf Hitler requested to be allowed to fight in the German army, even though was not a German citizen. Under no obligation to do so, he risked his life to save his adopted brothers in arms, was injured on the battlefield, and earned a medal for his courage.

When Donald Trump's educational deferments ran out, he sought a medical excuse not to go and fight in the Vietnam War. Trump had received military training at his elite private academy, but he was reluctant to put it into practice. Even though an initial medical examination found him physically fit for military duty, giving him A-1 status, a second medical examination conducted shortly before he was to be eligible for the draft lottery discovered a minor medical defect in his feet, enabling Trump to evade going to Vietnam. "Bone spurs," the doctor called it.

There's nothing wrong with people deciding not to join in a war that they disagree with, or to abstain from violence completely due to deeply held philosophical principles. That's not what appears to have motivated Donald Trump, however. There is no record of Trump taking part in any anti-war protest. He seems to simply have wanted to save his own skin, allowing other people to fight and die in his place.

Not all future presidential candidates made Trump's choice, of course. Secretary of State John Kerry volunteered to fight in Vietnam. So did Senator John McCain – not that this decision impresses Trump.

"He's not a war hero," Trump said of Senator McCain in 2015, shortly after declaring the beginning of his presidential campaign. "I like people who weren't captured."

It is true that John McCain had been a prisoner of war in Vietnam before beginning his political career, but his capture had nothing to do with a lack of heroism. His plane was struck by a missile over Hanoi. He broke both arms and one leg while ejecting from the plane, and landed in a lake. After being pulled ashore he was captured by North Vietnamese soldiers, who stabbed him with a bayonet and crushed his shoulder with a rifle butt. He was held prisoner for over five years, during which time he received minimal medical care and was repeatedly tortured. It is simply not plausible to claim that someone who was more of a "hero" could have somehow avoided this capture and imprisonment.

Trump's dismissal of John McCain's suffering in a prisoner of war camp was particularly cruel given Trump's enthusiasm for reinstating George W. Bush's programs of torture against prisoners of war, which were put to a stop under President Barack Obama. After hearing his blunt insult against a well-respected Republican U.S. Senator and former presidential candidate, most political pundits assumed that Trump's presidential campaign had destroyed itself, almost as soon as it began. The Republican Party, after all, prided itself upon showing conspicuous respect to military veterans, in word if not always in deed.

The pundits were soon proven wrong. Donald Trump's ratings in public opinion polls of likely Republican voters didn't decrease at all after the jab at McCain. In fact, Trump's ratings in a few of the polls began to rise.

These days, Trump seems to have changed his earlier reluctance to participate in violence. Now that he is too old to directly take part in war himself, he has become eager to send young men off to kill and be killed in war. His foreign policy is summed up with his phrase, "I would bomb the shit out of them!" This enthusiasm for extreme military action is one of the first points where the biographies of Donald Trump and Adolf Hitler begin to converge.

Certainly, the paths to power chosen by the two leaders were not the same. Trump has ascended to prominence through business, referring to himself as "the archetypal businessman". Hitler, lacking the inherited capital needed to make a quick launch into the business world, decided upon politics as his route to greatness. Whereas Trump declared himself an outside while exploiting a range of insider advantages available only to those born into wealth, Hitler claimed the status of a German cultural insider in spite of the fact that he began his life as a true outsider, with an identity defined by his disadvantages.

Although Hitler and Trump advanced through different professional spheres, they share in common the development of a particular oratory style. Both leaders have succeeded in building large followings through a bombastic, flamboyant approach to their speeches, exciting their audiences into explosive displays of emotion that sometimes erupt into violence. While Hitler's speeches are more formal than Trump's, both speakers use wild gestures and exaggerated facial expressions to keep their audiences enthralled. The speeches of both men use superlative language to convey a sense of urgent need, while avoiding wonky policy details.

Donald Trump certainly doesn't have the grammatical precision for which Barack Obama has become well known. He frequently abandons his thoughts halfway through as he speaks, talking in short sentence fragments that crudely hint at an idea rather than spelling it out in a logical way.

This fractured approach to language is a quality Trump shares with Hitler. Although he was known as an effective orator, Hitler's language was also awkward, like Trump's. Psychologist Walter Langer noted in his wartime Psychological Analysis of Adolf Hitler that, "On the whole, his speeches were sinfully long, badly structured and very repetitious. Some of them are positively painful to read, but nevertheless, when he delivered them they had an extraordinary effect upon his audiences." In the speeches of both Trump and Hitler, proper language isn't the point. In fact, the power of their public speaking seems to derive from a willingness to be flagrantly improper.

Donald Trump has become well-known for the excitement he derives from breaking the rules of acceptable speech. It has often been said that much of the power of Trump's speeches come from the fact that he says in public what many Americans believe in private, but are unwilling to say out loud. In 2015, at a time when most political observers believed that Trump had no chance of being elected President, the Washington Times, a deeply conservative newspaper, observed that, "Mr. Trump says what nearly everybody thinks, but is too fearful or polite to say. He says it in a rough and coarse way, which deserves rebuke, but rebuke wouldn't be necessary if other, housebroken politicians had the courage to say the things he says in a softer way."

Langer noted the same quality in Hitler's speeches. He wrote that, "somehow he always managed to say what the majority of the audiences were already secretly thinking but could not verbalize."

Above all else, Trump and Hitler both rely upon the power of emphatic assertion, not worrying about providing evidence for their claims of truth. They use overpowering confidence to cultivate a sense of trust within people listening to them. "Believe me," Trump tells his audiences, over and over again. They do.

Just as audiences of Americans are willing to believe Trump regardless of the factual and logical flaws in his speech, Germans in the 1930s were quite willing to believe Adolf Hitler's wildest assertions. "He was so convincing on the speaker's platform and appeared to be so sincere in what he said," Langer wrote, "that the majority of his listeners were ready to believe almost anything good about him because they wanted to believe it." As we all know now, this belief in Hitler's greatness was not merited, but at the time, it was difficult for Germans to question so convincing a performance.

Trump seems to believe in himself as much as his rank and file supporters do. He once declared to Jimmy Fallon, on The Tonight Show, that, "I think apologizing's a great thing, but you have to be wrong. I will absolutely apologize, sometime in the hopefully distant future, if I'm ever wrong."

It is possible that the similarities between the energetic speaking styles of Hitler and Trump are due to something more than mere happenstance. In 1990, Donald Trump's first wife, Ivana, divulged that her husband kept a collection of Hitler's speeches, titled My New Order, in a cabinet by his side of the bed. Marty Davis, an entertainment executive, confirmed that he had given

Trump a copy of the book.

When confronted about his dedication of a special place in his bedroom just for Hitler's speeches, Donald Trump claimed that it wasn't a big deal, because Davis was Jewish. Davis has responded by exposing the hollow nature of Trump's excuse. "I am his friend, but I'm not Jewish," Davis says.

The plainly false character of Trump's statements in cases such as this never seems to have a lasting impact on him. Over and over again, Trump has been caught telling flagrant lies, but these falsehoods have never harmed his political ascent. Trump's supporters seem not to care that he lies, perhaps because his lies are so flagrant. The lies are said with conviction, and what his supporters seek is a man of conviction rather than a man of truth.

Trump's repeated displays of his extreme wealth were supposed by many of his liberal critics to be a political vulnerability that would offend the economically-struggling Americans which Trump claimed as his political base. In actuality, the working class character of Trump supporters has simply been another distortion of the truth, one that most Americans continue to believe, even though election data clearly show it to be false. Most low income voters cast ballots in opposition to Trump on Election Day 2016, not for him. Trump's votes came mostly from middle class Americans aspiring to wealth, not from people struggling to get by.

To Trump's supporters, his displays of over-the-top, gaudy wealth were appealing, because they represented their own dreams of extreme luxury. Photographs of Trump's Manhattan penthouse apartment, in which every surface appears to be covered in gold leaf, may seem tasteless to professional designers, but Trump supporters aren't interested in tasteful restraint, because they dream of unrestrained luxury for themselves.

Such shameless flaunting of luxury is a personality characteristic that Donald Trump does not have in common with Adolf Hitler. Hitler was born into economic struggle, and sought to connect to working Germans through displays of personal austerity. Walter Lang explains that this gap between the ambitions of Hitler's supporters and Hitler's own supposedly frugal lifestyle cast Hitler in a sacred light. "The ordinary man in the street," Langer wrote, "cannot imagine a human being in Hitler's position not taking advantage of his opportunity. He can only imagine himself in the same position revelling [sic] in luxuries and yet here is Hitler who scorns them all. His only conclusion is that Hitler is not an ordinary mortal."

The position achieved by Trump is the polar opposite. Born into wealth, Trump's tasteless show of luxuriating in extravagance creates the appearance to middle class Americans that he actually is one of them, merely one step ahead of them in the march toward life of luxury that they deserve, a newcomer to his riches who is reveling in his good fortune. That this storyline is completely out of line with the facts of Trump's life is irrelevant. Trump makes it feel true.

Though he crafted a relatively frugal public persona, Hitler certainly believed in his own greatness. "It makes little difference whether the field be economics, education, foreign affairs, propaganda, movies, music, or women's dress. In each and every field he believes himself to be an unquestioned authority," Langer wrote about Hitler.

In late 2015, Michael D'Antonio, who had worked as Trump's authorized biographer, described an attitude of inflated self-worth that is remarkably similar to Hitler's. Just as Hitler believed that Germans were a genetically superior Aryan race, and that he was himself an exemplar of this excellence, Trump expressed to D'Antonio the belief in his own genetic superiority. Trump described himself as like a prize racehorse who was the result of generations of breeding between the best of the best.

"The racehorse theory of human development explains Trump's belief in his suitability for political leadership,"

D'Antonio wrote, "despite the fact that he has never held office. He's absolutely convinced that America's problems will be solved by his God-given management skills, bankruptcies notwithstanding. You are either born with superior qualities — the right DNA — or you are not."

Trump's belief in his inherent biological superiority veers at times into a messianic self-image. In the spring of 2016, he announced to a crowd of fossil fuel industry executives gathered in Bismarck, North Dakota, that "I will give you everything. I will give you what you've been looking for for 50 years. I'm the only one." At the Republican National Convention later that year, he depicted the United States as teetering on the brink of calamity before proudly announcing to the nation that "I alone can fix it."

This feeling of being a special person chosen by destiny was also a dominant factor in Hitler's personality. Just as Trump believes that only he can Make America Great Again, Hitler believed that he alone could lead Germany to greatness. Peter Ross Range, author of 1924: The Year That Made Hitler, writes, "No resemblance has been stronger than Trump's claim that he 'alone' could rescue America from its misery. Hitler famously conjoured the model of 'the genius, the great man' who alone held the key to a country's destiny... Hitler was building the case for the 'Fuhrer principle' – a belief in the iron infallibility of the leader. It was an elaborate, historically wrought version of the 'I alone' principle."

Both Trump and Hitler manifested their personal cults of exceptionalism through large construction projects which they insisted on being named after themselves. Describing Hitler's pathological need for these monuments to himself, Langer commented, "Everything must be huge and befitting as a monument to the honor of Hitler. His idea of a permanent building is one which will endure at least a thousand years. His highways must be known as 'Hitler Highways'."

As we hear this description of Hitler's need to see his face and name spread far and wide, the similarities to Donald Trump are obvious. Trump has not only placed his name on Trump Tower in Manhattan, but has spread the Trump Tower brand around the world. Even this level of recognition isn't enough for Trump, who has put his name on products that have nothing to do with his original specialty of real estate: Trump steaks, Trump clothing, all the way to the infamous Trump University. Ana Swanson at the Washington Post notes that "Trump's penchant for deploying his name has been a successful marketing strategy, but it also appears to satisfy a deeper desire for fame and accomplishment."

Yet, for both Trump and Hitler, a public "braggadocious" persona may conceal a deeper feeling of shame, creating a psychological conflict that exhibits itself in a strange combination of compulsive disobedience with an obsession drive to be privately shamed. An unexpected biographical parallel between the two in this vein was suggested just days before Trump's inauguration as President in January of 2017. Three top U.S. intelligence agencies came together to present a report to both President Barack Obama and President Elect Trump, providing evidence that Russian spies had, on direct orders from dictator Vladimir Putin, hacked into computer systems held by both the Democratic National Committee and the Republican National Committee. While the Russians had kept secret the information they found on Republican computers, perhaps for later use, the Russian government released information it had stolen from Democratic computers, in order to cripple the presidential campaign of Hillary Clinton and throw the election to Donald Trump.

A few days after a declassified, partial summary of these reports was released to the American people, a leaked copy of another report. This report, made public on the site Buzzfeed, was written by Christopher Steele, a former spy with the British intelligence agency MI6. It alleged that Trump had cooperated with the Russian cyberattack in order to gain advantage the presidential election, that he had served as an informant to Russian spies for at least eight years, and that Russian spies had assembled a substantial body of highly embarrassing and legally compromising material about Trump so that the government of Russia could blackmail him after his election as President.

Among this body of material, Steele's report alleged, were videotapes of Donald Trump engaged in unusual sexual activities in a variety settings, recorded on many occasions over a long period of time. Describing one of these videotapes, the existence of which Steele claimed was verified by two different sources, the report states, "There were other aspects to Trump's engagement with the Russian authorities. One which had borne fruit for them was to exploit Trump's personal obsessions and sexual perversion in order to obtain suitable 'kompromat' (compromising material) on him. According to Source D, where s/he had been present, Trump's (perverted) conduct in Moscow included hiring the presidential suite of the Ritz Carlton Hotel where he knew President and Mrs Obama (whom he hated) had stayed on one of their official trips to Russia, and defiling the bed where they had slept by employing a number of prostitutes to perform a 'golden showers' (urination) show in front of him. The hotel was known to be under FSB control with microphones and concealed cameras in all the main rooms to record anything they wanted to."

For all of his faults, Adolf Hitler was never accused of being a spy for a foreign government. However, Hitler was repeatedly accused of having a masochistic sexual tendency which manifested itself in having women perform golden showers, and more, on him. Walter Langer repeated these allegations as they were told to him by Otto Strasser, a high-level Nazi defector. "His perversion has quite a different nature which few have guessed. He is an extreme masochist who derives sexual pleasure from having a woman squat over him while she urinates or defecates on his face," Langer wrote.

At present, the truth of these allegations against Trump and Hitler is not certain. However, it is striking that both men have been accused by intelligence officials of the same uncommon sexual fetish. These particular kinds of claims are rarely made about national leaders. That both Trump and Hitler have been accused by spy agencies of being sexually obsessed with human waste suggests that, at the very least, there is something about their political personas that invites such speculation.

Photo by Gage Skidmore

CHAPTER 3:
THE HISTORY OF WEIMAR GERMANY AND THE USA TODAY

Whether Donald Trump, as an individual, is similar to Adolf Hitler is not the ultimate concern for American voters. It is the social movement that Trump represents that matters most.

All of the cruel destruction that Hitler inflicted would have been impossible without huge numbers of other people, in almost every segment of German society, willing to do his bidding. In another time, in another place, in another culture, Adolf Hitler would have been unknown to history, confined to a marginal role, his irrational fury unable to harm anyone but the few people immediately around him.

To understand whether the threat to peace and freedom posed by Donald Trump is anything similar to the threat that was posed by Adolf Hitler, it is necessary to consider how much the United States today has in common with the Weimar Republic of Germany, from which Hitler and the Nazi Party rose to power. The question of whether the USA is likely to allow Trump to run away with power as Hitler did in Germany.

This comparison brings cause for hope, because there are some profound differences between the United States today and Germany in the 1920s and 1930s.

The most fundamental difference has to do with national stability. For generations, the United States has been a well-established nation, with a solid and stable identity. Not since the Civil War, a century and a half ago, has this identity faced a serious challenge, either from within or without.

Germany, on the other hand, was barely more than an abstract concept when Hitler rose to power. During the Weimar Republic, the national government was weak, with the leaders of Germany's constituent states constantly testing central authority. Germany had been a region of separate sovereign states for centuries, and then a loose confederation before its brief status as an empire.

During Hitler's young life, many Germans didn't live within the borders of Germany at all, and many of those who lived within Germany didn't really think of themselves as Germans. There were Prussians and Bavarians, Slavs and Poles, and then there were Jews. Hitler's assertion that he was, though born in Austria, a true German, was always in dispute, although the dispute went underground after the Anschluss.

Germany was still in a process of becoming a culturally authentic when Hitler made his way onto the political stage. As a result, many of the basic tenets of how Germany could be governed were still up for debate.

In the United States, we have lived under the same Constitution for well over two hundred years. That Constitution has been amended, and our understanding of how the Constitution should be applied has shifted, but the core legal principles of American government have remained the same since shortly after the Revolution of 1776. The longevity of our Bill of Rights and other liberties places a more substantial barrier in the way of a would-be American despot than what Hitler had to surmount.

The democratic idealism that held the Weimar Republic together consisted of mere wisps compared to the marble columns of democracy in the United States. In the years when Hitler scrambled to national prominence, it was not at all uncommon for German politicians to openly sneer at the weakness of democracy. It may be an exaggeration to say that aspiring dictators were a dime a dozen, but not much of one. Many Weimar Germans were even seeking the restoration of monarchy.

Unlike the Germans of the early 20th century, we Americans do not live in a culture where the display of a strong man's power places him above and beyond the normal system of rules. In our country, no one is above the law. In the Weimar Republic, the law bent in different ways for different people.

If an American organized an armed rebellion against the U.S. federal government, that person would be punished harshly, perhaps even executed for treason. Even the Bundy brothers, who couldn't manage to do more than establish an armed occupation of a government bird sanctuary gift shop which was closed for the winter, faced criminal trial on felony conspiracy charges. It took a jury of their peers to let them off the hook. When Hitler attempted a much more violent revolution, it was the legal system itself that intervened to allowed him to do easy time in a comfortable prison rather than being shot by a firing squad.

There is one sphere of American society, however, in which disdain for liberty, equality and the rule of law equals that seen in Weimar Germany: The realm of popular entertainment. Donald Trump has been practicing political tactics in this arena for years, as the star of a pair of unreal reality shows on TV – Apprentice and Celebrity

Apprentice.

Fact and fantasy are blended in theatrically compelling ways on these shows, in which Trump portrays a fictional version of himself: A chief executive with absolute power.

Magician Penn Jillette, who appeared as a contestant on one of these shows, explained that, "No one can tell you the rules of Celebrity Apprentice. No one. Donald Trump just does what he wants, which is mostly pontificating to people who are sucking up to him."

On his TV shows, Trump has no anxious investors, no board of directors to answer to, nobody to check his authority in any way. No one on these shows has any power at all to contest his catch phrase declaration of authority: "You're fired!"

The actual business ventures featured on The Apprentice are very small in scale. Contestants are put in charge of minor tasks like organizing a small reception, running a retail store for a few days, or selling candy on the street. These businesses are only significant as proving grounds for people who aspire to the servitude of apprenticeship to Trump. The contrived drama of Apprentice is designed to exhibit the subservience of all before the power of Trump, much as Nazi rallies were designed to display the absolute authority of Hitler over everyone involved.

In the actual business of The Apprentice, Trump is far from all-powerful. He has to answer to network executives and advertisers. In the real world of The Apprentice, Trump himself has been fired.

Ironically, it was Trump's disparaging comments about immigrants that caused him to lose his job and be replaced by an immigrant. Arnold Schwarzenegger is hosting Celebrity Apprentice in the current season.

Trump, by becoming President of the United States, has merely moved onto a larger stage. Trump has smoothly transitioned this persona from reality TV to the White House. While other candidates look visibly uncomfortable trading their power suits for nylon jackets when talking to working class crowds, Trump casually mismatches class symbols by wearing a baseball hats with expensive suits. He is a billionaire populist, who appeals to the masses not in spite of, but because of, his elite status. He does not promise a return of power directly to average citizens, or a revitalization of the democratic process. Instead, he promises to wield absolute power on behalf of America. For people who feel powerless, and see little prospect of becoming powerful in the future, this promise is appealing.

"You know, I get greedy. I want money, money. Now, I'm going to - I'll tell you what we're going to do, right? We get greedy, right?" Trump told his followers after his victory in the Nevada caucus. "Now we're going to get greedy for the United States. We're going to grab and grab and grab." Through statements like these, Trump gives permission to his followers to express desires that are perceived as shameful in other settings.

The collective joy experienced by people in the crowds at Trump rallies comes from the release of dark emotions that Americans are ordinarily encouraged to suppress. Barely controlled anger is a feature shared by the popular movements behind both Hitler and Trump. Donald Trump's campaign rallies have become infamous for their eruptions of mob violence against anti-Trump protesters. At times, Trump seems to encourage the attacks. After one rally, at which Trump supporters repeatedly attacked an African-American man while Trump himself shouted, "get him out of here," the candidate was unapologetic. "Maybe he should have been roughed up, because it was absolutely disgusting what he was doing," he told a reporter.

At another rally, when a protester was forced out of the arena, Trump roared to the crowd, "The guards are being very gentle with him. I'd like to punch him in the face, I'll tell you that!" Thousands of supporters shouted their approval, and then Trump told them, "You know what they used to do to a guy like that in a place like this? They'd be carried out on a stretcher, folks."

The violent rage within crowds of Trump supporters had its equivalent in Hitler's Nazi gatherings. Hitler himself bragged about it, writing in Mein Kampf, about a particular outburst, "There was a hail of shouts, there were violent clashes in the hall, a handful of the most faithful war comrades and other supporters battled with the disturbers… Communists and Socialists… and only little by little were able to restore order. I was able to go on speaking."

Of course, the Nazis weren't just violent in the arenas. They were bloody out on the streets as well. Nazi militias engaged in armed clashes with gangs from other political parties. We've seen hints of this kind of brutality from the supporters of Donald Trump – such as when he inspired one of his fans to beat a homeless Hispanic man with a metal pole. The attacker told police afterwards that "Donald Trump was right, all these illegals need to be deported," although the victim was a U.S. citizen.

After Election Day, the threats and violence by Trump supporters only grew worse. At Texas State University, Trump supporters distributed leaflets threatening to "arrest and torture" university officials as punishment for allowing respect for diversity on campus. In Missouri, a man purposefully drove his truck into a middle of a crowd of people protesting against Trump. A protest in Ohio was broken up after a Trump supporter tackled a young person speaking out in criticism of the President-Elect. In just the first week after Election Day, there were over 400 such incidents, according to the Southern Poverty Law Center.

A month before Inauguration Day, Trump dropped his claims that his supporters were being unfairly accused of violence. Speaking to a rally of his fans, Trump spoke in adoring tones while describing the attacks and intimidation inflicted by his supporters upon his critics. "You people were vicious, violent, screaming, 'Where's the wall? We want the wall!' Screaming, 'Prison! Prison! Lock her up!' I mean you are going crazy. I mean, you were nasty and mean and vicious and you wanted to win, right?" Then, the façade rose back up, as Trump claimed that there were no post-election troubles. "Now, you're mellow and you're cool," he said, "and you're not nearly as vicious or violent, right? Because we won, right?"

In response, at that same rally, Trump supporters threw objects at journalists covering the event. One Trump supporter at the rally screamed that Hillary Clinton should be tortured with waterboarding.

Attacks by Trump supporters have been deplorable, but Nazi violence in Germany took on quite a different scale. Kristallnacht didn't take place until five years after Adolf Hitler seized power, but there were Nazi brutalities all over Germany while the Nazis were on the rise. So far, we aren't seeing that much widespread violence from mobs of Trump supporters, although many threats have been made. Trump himself warned that if he wasn't given the Republican nomination, there would be riots in the street.

The United States doesn't have a might-makes-right political culture in which political parties establish squads of armed, uniformed goons. It wasn't just the Nazi Party that had these in Weimar Germany.

Political violence wasn't restricted to the attacks and intimidation by individuals or gangs, either. The German political atmosphere in the 1920s and 1930s was extremely volatile. Attempted coups d'etat were not uncommon.

A devastated economy was one factor that fueled this violence. There are serious, systemic problems in the American economy in our time. However, the state of the economy in the Weimar Republic was far worse than the state of the American economy is now.

Toward the end of the republic, inflation had made German currency practically worthless. Unemployment was pervasive – and even those Germans who had work couldn't pay for the necessities of life. Bread lines stretched out into the streets. The economic crisis was so grave that German society was on the verge of falling apart. On top of the global Great Depression, Germany was compelled to pay crippling reparations to the countries it had attacked in World War I.

Germany's military defeat was the other major factor that contributed to the roiling brutality of political life in the Weimar Republic. Donald Trump is fond of saying that America doesn't win anything any more (in fact, he's been saying this since the 1980s), but the losses Trump cites are microscopic in comparison to what Germany dealt with in 1918.

World War I had been savage for every nation involved, with extremely high numbers of fatalities and terribly wounded men. The fighting was more intense than anything anyone had ever seen before, amplified by horrible new weapons. For Germany, to have lost the war after all this suffering was profoundly traumatic. Huge numbers of soldiers returned to Germans towns and cities in a state of profound psychological disturbance. The entire society was a wreck. The United States has suffered nothing of this scale in recent times.

In historical fact, there are strong differences between Weimar Germany and the United States today. However, there are strong similarities between the way that Weimar Germans felt about the condition of their society and the way that many Americans today perceive the status of their nation. Emotional subjectivity beats objective reality every time.

"We're a third world nation," Trump writes. Of course, this is a silly, ignorant thing to say. The United States is an economic superpower, and Americans on the whole live in great luxury compared to the conditions endured by much of the rest of the world. Only an out-of-touch billionaire could believe that the conditions in America are anything like those of a genuine third world nation.

What is true is that Americans feel economically deprived. They feel alienated in their workplaces, where schemes of corporate efficiency increasingly squeeze the humanity out of their labor. They feel simultaneously dazzled and disoriented by the rapid changes wrought by racing developments in digital technology.

Republicans in particular feel unsettled by cultural changes such as the embrace of equal rights for homosexuals and the slow decline of American Christianity. What for many other Americans feels like a liberation seems to them a terrifying dissolution of the bedrock upon which civilization is founded.

Furthermore, for American racists, who are not insubstantial in number, the presidency of Barack Obama has provoked a psychological crisis. They have been confronted, year after year, with a competent, respected man with dark skin who has been able to repeatedly outmaneuver his light-skinned opponents. In the minds of racists, such a thing ought not to be possible. Obama is to politics as Jesse Owens was to athletics.

Some racists have responded by softening their hatred. Most, however, have merely twisted their anger into new, more uncomfortable forms. To compensate for the unavoidable political supremacy of a successful African-American, they have developed large numbers of outlandish conspiracy theories that, if they were not so collective, would be regarded as symptoms of insanity.

Republican social networks are flooded with extreme stories of abuse of power and looming calamity. These stories claim that Barack Obama has purposefully allowed Muslim terrorists into the United States, carrying carrying nuclear suitcase bombs that are about to be detonated. It doesn't matter that these stories have been repeated over and over throughout President Obama's two terms in office, and have never come true or been substantiated in any form. To many Republican voters, they feel true.

The stories tell of Obama's plan to introduce the Ebola

virus, a potent symbol of African identity gone out of control, to the United States. They tell of secret concentration camps that have been built across the United States by the Federal Emergency Management Agency. They tell of the secret movement of American soldiers across the United States and military training exercises that will soon impose martial law. They simultaneously tell of strict Islamic sharia law being imposed, and of ministers being forced to marry gay couples. There have even been widespread rumors spread among Republican voters of guillotines being secretly installed in communities across America, to be used in the slaughter of American Christians that the rumors say is soon to come.

In a cultural context where such wild tales are given credence, Trump's vision of an America that has been defeated doesn't require consistency in either logic or facts. It merely needs to represent an emotional truth. Trump's supporters genuinely feel that their country has gone to hell in a handbasket, and requires a powerful hand to guide it back into victory, solvency and righteousness.

Trump shares in this emotionally-driven cognitive dissonance. Within a single paragraph, Trump writes that, "We have to take it back, we have to take our country back. We've lost our jobs, we've lost our money," and that "I have some of the great assets of the world." These two assertions of truth, that Donald Trump possesses "great assets" and that "we" have lost "our money", are rationally incompatible, but that doesn't matter to Trump and his supporters. What matters is that both assertions feel true, and that they point to a fundamental wrong in the world that must be put right: That America is a wealthy nation that nonetheless feels impoverished.

Among Republicans, the source of this conflict is the combination of the reality of economic struggle with two of their political party's central creeds: 1) that the United States is the greatest nation on Earth, and 2) that the

United States is a meritocracy. If the United States really was both the greatest nation on Earth and a meritocracy, then there wouldn't be any economic problems for any hard-working American.

What most Americans actually experience is that their hard work often doesn't pay off in the end. Since the Great Recession, the wealthiest Americans have grown ever more wealthy, while the rest of America, including not just the poor but also the middle class, has been forced to work longer hours for less money. What's more, for decades, worker productivity has been rising, while wages have been falling. This combination of statistics shows that investors and business owners, such as Trump, have been squeezing wealth from workers in an increasingly raw deal.

Many American workers, however, don't want to blame American financial elites for their economic struggles. That's because their sense of individual power relies upon the feeling that they can improve their economic condition through sheer effort, regardless of the obstacles. Without this belief, many working Americans simply wouldn't feel able to go on.

As a result, the message of Donald Trump holds a special appeal. Instead of acknowledging that it's people like himself, within the USA, that have taken wealth from working Americans, Trump blames outsiders. He blames immigrants. He blames China. He blames Barack Obama for failing to stand up to China. He declares that American workers need a strongman to get tough and demand a better deal, when in fact, it's the strongmen of American business who have stripped the wealth out of working Americans' lives in the first place.

It's politically appealing to blame outsiders for working Americans' economic problems, because outsiders can be dealt with more simply, with a posture of toughness. Admitting that the problem may lie within the American system itself requires people to acknowledge flaws that are closer to home, when they are already feeling vulnerable.

The fractured, irrational vision of Trump's economic scapegoating is strikingly similar to the belief harbored by many Germans of Hitler's generation that the German military had been "stabbed in the back" at the end of World War I. These Germans, many of whom, like Hitler, were in the field when their country was forced to surrender, had an ardent faith in the superiority of the German military. Lacking a broader vision of the war, they only saw that their individual units seemed to be holding their own against the enemy.

When the order came to stand down, and the news arrived that Germany was surrendering under humiliating terms, German soldiers were outraged. They refused to believe that their own military had been defeated, that their own fighting had been in vain, that they had risked their lives, enduring terror and sacrifice for years, for nothing. It was easier for them to find someone else, someone non-German, to blame.

So it was that Adolf Hitler, and many others in his position, found the psychological power of redirecting their frustration against Jews. It was easier for them to believe that they had been betrayed by a cabal of Jews that secretly controlled Germany than to believe that Germany had failed itself by launching a war that it could not sustain. The Jews, it seemed, would be easy to defeat. There were more Germans than Jews, after all.

For a while, the anti-Semitic fantasy energized the Germans who believed in it. It brought the Nazis to power and enabled a burst of military revitalization. However, in the end, the pursuit of phantom Jewish puppet masters brought Germany to disaster again.

It is too early to say whether the United States will be wrecked by an irrational pursuit of convenient scapegoats in the way that Germany was ruined by its irrational hunger for Jewish blood. What we can observe is that the presidential campaign of Donald Trump has identified several vulnerable populations as convenient scapegoats, and is readying Americans for a purge. As this edition moves to publication, President Trump confirms that he is preparing to prohibit Muslims from international travel, and is preparing to expel millions of Hispanics from the USA.

If this sounds ominous, consider what's at stake in this historical moment. Nations all over the Earth suffered terribly during World War II, but the weaponry now held in the militaries of the world makes the armaments used by the Nazis seem insignificant.

When Adolf Hitler took power, the German military was much weaker than that of its European rivals. Donald Trump has inherited a military that is several times stronger than all the other militaries on the planet combined – and he plans to make it even more powerful.

The threat posed by the current stockpiles of nuclear weapons apparently isn't enough for Trump. In December 2016, Trump revealed that he wants to go back to the Cold War policy of building more nuclear weapons than could possibly be of use in even the most terrible nuclear war. "The United States must greatly strengthen and expand its nuclear capability," he said. When he challenged on whether building more nuclear weapons could cause international tensions, Trump replied, "Let it be an arms race. We will outmatch them at every pass and outlast them all."

What's more, Trump has declared that he's open to the idea of nuclear weapons proliferation around the world, allowing countries such as South Korea and Japan to build nuclear weapons stockpiles. "Wouldn't you rather, in a certain sense, have Japan have nuclear weapons?" Trump asks.

As much as the Allies worried about the possibility, Adolf Hitler was never able to develop nuclear weapons. As President of the United States, Trump has thousands of nuclear weapons at his disposal, each one many times more powerful than the atomic bombs the American military dropped on Hiroshima and Nagasaki.

If Donald Trump were to lose his temper, made to feel that he had come out the loser in a negotiation, or decide on a whim to improvise…

…that could be the end for us all.

Photo by Gage Skidmore

CHAPTER 4:
IDEOLOGIES OF THE
NAZIS AND DONALD TRUMP

"We're going to have to do things that we never did before... and certain things will be done that we never thought would happen in this country." – Donald Trump

That there are differences between the biographical and historical contexts of Adolf Hitler's rise to power and Donald Trump's presidential campaign is reassuring. The similarities between the ideologies crafted by the Nazis and Donald Trump, however, are disturbing.

At the core of these similarities is an extreme nationalism, fueled by xenophobia. The particular outsiders loathed by Hitler and Trump are different, but the tenor of their loathing is the same.

The Nazi rise to power was fueled by an ancient ideology of antipathy toward Jews, constructed out of an elaborate system of delusions of persecution. Among these delusions was the blood libel.

The blood libel was the false belief that Jews routinely kidnap Christian children in order to kill them and drain them of blood, which is subsequently used for secret Jewish rituals. Although the blood libel predated the Third Reich by hundreds of years, its impact reached an unprecedented scale under the Nazis, who used it as an excuse for the barbarities of the Holocaust.

There is no evidence that Donald Trump has ever uttered the ancient blood libel against Jews in any form. He has been accused of indulging in negative stereotypes of Jews on occasion, but when Trump is antisemitic, he is not blatant about it. Instead, Trump speaks in antisemitic codes. For example, when, at the end of the 2016 election season, Trump declared that a secret cabal of international bankers had rigged the election against him, he was invoking a centuries-old slur against Jews.

On another occasion, Trump republished an image with a picture of Hillary Clinton in front of a pile of money, along with Star of David over which the phrase "most corrupt candidate ever" was superimposed. It was soon discovered that Trump had obtained the picture directly from an American Nazi. Even after it became public that the image he used had Nazi origins, Trump angrily insisted that he would publish the image all over again.

A disturbingly large number of Trump's tweets have their origins in American Nazi circles. One Trump tweet, an image listing false black-on-white homicide statistics, was originally designed by a Nazi who a swastika for an avatar. This Nazi Trump supporter is very open about his affection for Adolf Hitler, declaring in public that, "We should have listened to the Austrian chap with the little moustache."

Trump has engaged in many equivalents of the blood libel against non-Jewish minority groups. Over the last decade, for example, Trump has played a prominent role in the spread of an intentional lie about American Muslims, one designed to malign Muslims as a category and Barack Obama as an individual. You've heard of this, of course: It's the conspiracy theory that Barack Obama wasn't really born in the United States, and that he doesn't have a genuine birth certificate, or his birth certificate has been doctored to create the false impression that Obama is an American citizen.

On Twitter, Donald Trump declared that "An 'extremely credible source' has called my office and told me that @BarackObama's birth certificate is a fraud." Elsewhere, Trump insisted that President Barack Obama, "doesn't have a birth certificate. He may have one, but there's something on that, maybe religion, maybe it says he is a Muslim. I don't know. Maybe he doesn't want that." Over and over again, for years, Trump told this story to anyone who would listen to it.

There are several manifestations of this conspiracy theory, and Donald Trump seems receptive to all of them. In one version, Barack Obama was born in Kenya, and was raised there as a boy to be a radical follower of Islam. In another version, Barack Obama was born in Cuba, and raised there as a boy to be a radical follower of Communism. In some versions, Barack Obama is alleged to be both a radical Communist and a fundamentalist Muslim, even though those ideologies are inherently incompatible.

In most versions of the story, Barack Obama is alleged to be a secret agent, trained to go deep undercover in the United States, to run for President, and then let the enemies of America cross the border to wage a campaign of destruction from within the USA. None of the people who have promoted these conspiracy theories have explained why, after two complete Obama terms, America hasn't been destroyed yet.

Barack Obama isn't Muslim. He showed the public his birth certificate years ago. These facts haven't deflated the blood libel of Obama as the bloodthirsty Muslim, though. That's because those who believe in the conspiracy theory are compelled by an emotionally-shaped idea that can withstand practically any rational refutation: the belief that only Christians of pure European ancestry are qualified to lead the nation. The promotion of that white supremacist belief, in itself, makes for a compelling convergence between the ideologies of the Nazis and the Republican Party.

The parallels don't end there, however. Trump has repeated a new anti-Muslim blood libel, a tall tale about thousands of Muslims cheering in New Jersey as the Twin Towers of the World Trade Center were destroyed by terrorists on September 11, 2001. Trump has insisted that, "I watched when the World Trade Center came tumbling down. And I watched in Jersey City, New Jersey, where thousands and thousands of people were cheering as that building was coming down. Thousands of people were cheering." Ben Carson, a retired neurosurgeon who Trump has decided should run the Department of Housing and Urban Development despite Carson's complete lack of professional experience in the field, has repeated the story.

There is no evidence at all of anyone cheering the fall of the Twin Towers across the river in New Jersey, much less a crowd of thousands of American Muslims holding an impromptu party in the streets. Furthermore, Donald Trump wasn't in Jersey City at the time that he claims he saw huge crowds there cheering the terrorist attack against the United States.

Later, trying to defend his story, Trump said that he had seen the Jersey City Muslim celebrations of the September 11 attacks on a television news report. Journalists have scoured all their stockpiles of footage from that day, however, and no one has been able to find any evidence that any such television broadcast ever took place.

Of course, it's not a complete lie to say that there are Muslims who want to commit acts of terrorist violence in the United States. There are a few. Their numbers, however, are extremely small. The actual risk of death by a

Muslim terrorist attack in the United States is almost zero. The average annual number of people killed in the USA by Muslim terrorists is just two. Yes, that's right, two per year.

Every year, more people in the United States are killed by cows than are killed by Islamic militants.

What's more, the United States has suffered from terrorist attacks that have nothing to do with Islam at all. Timothy McVeigh and the Unibomber weren't Muslims, but they killed viciously nonetheless.

The blood libel made by Donald Trump and other opportunistic Republican politicians is that American Muslims are always just a hair's width from conducting a terrorist attack, and celebrate violence against Americans whenever it happens. "Trump and Carson here are playing a particularly nasty game," writes Benjamin Wittes, Senior Fellow in Governance Studies at that Brookings Institution. "They are fabulists of the worst kind - that is to say they are fabulists in the malicious denigration of others. They are making things up to stoke hatred and intolerance; they are little different in that regard from those who peddled lies about black men raping white women in the old South or those those who made up and stuck by blood libels in old Europe. These type of lies have consequences."

It wasn't just Jews that Adolf Hitler and the Nazis crafted libels against, of course. Another one of their targets were Democratic Socialists – a relatively liberal political party in the Weimar Republic. The Nazis accused them of seeking to destroy religion, and so cast themselves as the great defenders of Christianity.

"My feelings as a Christian point me to my Lord and Savior as a fighter," Hitler said. "We tolerate no one in our ranks who attacks the ideas of Christianity... in fact our movement is Christian." His opponents, warned Hitler, were radical atheists who had no respect for the role of religion in public life. "We were convinced that the people needs and requires this faith. We have therefore undertaken the fight against the atheistic movement," he said.

Donald Trump adopts a pose as the great defender of the Christian faith that is similar to Hitler's. "I'm proud to be a Christian, and as president I will not allow Christianity to be consistently attacked and weakened," he has declared. The fact that Christianity remains the most powerful religion in the United States doesn't seem to impact Trump's determination that it is in grave peril of being destroyed.

Among the supposed threats to Christianity that demands special attention from the President of the United States is the lack of adequate promotion of Christmas on the disposable coffee cups handed out at some coffee chains. Trump was outraged to hear that Starbucks coffee cups didn't offer a specific holiday greeting last year. "Did you read about Starbucks?" he angrily demanded of a crowd of supporters last December. "No more 'Merry Christmas' at Starbucks. No more. Maybe we should boycott Starbucks."

It seems silly, but Donald Trump's verbal assault against Starbucks coffee cups is part of a larger right wing narrative that re-emerges every year. It's a story of a War on Christmas.

The idea is that Christians are under siege in America. Socialist secular liberals are supposed to be on a campaign to wipe out the Christian religion, using department stores and coffee shops to do it. Every year, conservative Christian groups come out with lists of large businesses who are complicit in this supposed ideological assault. Their offense: In their advertisements and store displays in November and December, they don't use the word "Christmas" enough.

Christianity is in decline in the United States. Year after year, fewer people identify themselves as Christians, and more define themselves as unaffiliated to any religion. In reality, this change is part of a spontaneous shift away from a monolithic American cultural identity based on obedience and tradition, toward an American identity more associated with experimentation, innovation and diversity. Donald Trump and his supporters don't see it that way, however. They perceive the change as the consequence of a centralized conspiracy by secretive elites, manipulating society away from acts of Christian worship by purposefully eliminating commercial messages with the phrase, "Merry Christmas".

Donald Trump's ideology is similar to that of the Nazis in that he perceives his culture, that of conservative, European-American Christianity, to be under siege. It isn't just secular liberals who are at the gates of Trump's cultural citadel, however. When he looks out from his fortress, Trump sees an army of dirty Mexicans coming to take away his wealth.

Trump began his presidential campaign with a volley of insults against Hispanics in the United States. In his announcement speech, he declared, "When Mexico sends its people, they're not sending the best. They're sending people that have lots of problems and they're bringing those problems. They're bringing drugs, they're bringing crime. They're rapists and some, I assume, are good people, but I speak to border guards and they're telling us what we're getting."

Trump wasn't the first person to complain about the cultural impurities brought into the United States by immigrants from Mexico. What most people don't realize is that Adolf Hitler was an early critic of the idea of an open border between the Mexico and the United States.

In Mein Kampf, Adolf Hitler wrote that, "Whenever Aryans have mingled their blood with that of an inferior race the result has been the downfall of the people who were the standard-bearers of a higher culture. In North America, where the population is prevalently Teutonic, and where those elements intermingled with the inferior race only to a very small degree, we have a quality of mankind and a civilization which are different from those of Central and South America. In these latter countries the immigrants--who mainly belonged to the Latin races—mated with the aborigines, sometimes to a very large extent indeed. In this case we have a clear and decisive example of the effect produced by the mixture of races. But in North America the Teutonic element, which has kept its racial stock pure and did not mix it with any other racial stock, has come to dominate the American Continent and will remain master of it as long as that element does not fall a victim to the habit of adulterating its blood."

Reading these words from Adolf Hitler, the ideological link between Trump and the Nazi Party comes into focus. Hitler hoped that the Nazi Party purge of non-German immigrants would be modeled upon America's creation of strong borders to keep people from Latin America out. Hitler continued, "I realize fully that nobody likes to hear these things. But it would be difficult to find anything more illogical or more insane than our contemporary laws in regard to State citizenship. At present there exists one State which manifests at least some modest attempts that show a better appreciation of how things ought to be done in this matter. It is not, however, in our model German Republic but in the U.S.A. that efforts are made to conform at least partly to the counsels of commonsense. By refusing immigrants to enter there if they are in a bad state of health, and by excluding certain races from the right to become naturalized as citizens, they have begun to introduce principles similar to those on which we wish to ground the People's State."

Hitler, it seems, would strongly approve of Donald Trump's plan to expel 11 million Hispanics, and to build a gigantic border wall to separate the United States from the rest of the world.

Trump's vision of a purified America doesn't exclude only Hispanics. He also has proposed a ban on travel by all

Muslims, prohibiting them from entering the United States. Trump would even outlaw Muslim American citizens from coming back into the United States after driving into Canada to see Niagara Falls. Trump sees no half measures in his campaign for the cultural purification of America, but calls his plan "a total and complete shutdown" of Muslim freedom of movement into the United States.

In his demand for a complete border shutdown, Trump depicts Muslims as foreigners. In fact, Muslims have been in the United States for as long as there has been a United States. Historical records show that Muslims were among those who fought for independence from England in 1776.

There is a strong vein of racism in Trump's denial of the deep historical role of Muslims throughout American history. Today, most Muslims in the United States are African-American. Anti-Muslim measures are thus a way to lash out at African-American communities.

It's particularly ironic that Donald Trump is now leading an authoritarian Christian campaign to ban Muslims from entering the United States when, for generations, it was authoritarian Christians who demanded the right to bring Muslims into the United States without restriction.

Of course, back then, the Muslims were brought into the United States as property. They were brought into the United States, by force, as slaves.

The United States is like the Weimar Republic in that it carries the burden of a long, cruel history of racism and oppression of cultural minorities. The honored marble monuments of Washington DC were built by enslaved human beings. America's unique popular music was born out of the isolation and despair of racial segregation and oppression in Jim Crow America.

Americans like to think of these problems as mere history, something that their nation has moved beyond. In February 2016, however, the Trump for President campaign provided an astonishing reminder that the USA is not a post-racism society after all.

It began when David Duke, a prominent white supremacist and former Grand Wizard of the Ku Klux Klan expressed his enthusiastic support for the Trump campaign. Duke, who had previously declared that "Our clear goal must be the advancement of the white race and separation of the white and black races. This goal must include the freeing of the American media and government from subservient Jewish interests," now urged his neoNazi supporters to sign up to volunteer at the nearest Trump for President campaign office. "Go in there, you're gonna meet people who are going to have the same kind of mindset that you have," Duke told them.

When Trump was confronted by a reporter about this endorsement by the KKK leader, he refused to distance himself from Duke. Trump, who had never hesitated to slam Muslims, Mexicans, women, or gays, expressed a sudden reluctance to rush to judgment of the leader of a violent white nationalist organization, saying, "Just so you understand, I don't know anything about David Duke, OK? I don't know anything about what you're even talking about with white supremacy or white supremacists. So I don't know. I mean, I don't know - did he endorse me or what's going on? Because I know nothing about David Duke. I know nothing about white supremacists. And so you're asking me a question that I'm supposed to be talking about people that I know nothing about."

Trump pretended that he didn't know much about David Duke. However, in public comments 16 years before, Trump had acknowledged his familiarity with David Duke, and had properly identified Duke as a leader of racist organizations. It isn't easy to simply forget a Nazi extremist like David Duke.

Over the very same weekend that he received the support of the KKK, Trump decided to forward a quote from Fascist dictator Benito Mussolini to his followers.

The quote referred to the need for strong political leaders who are willing to feast upon the more vulnerable members of society: "It is better to live one day as a lion than 100 years as a sheep."

That the quote came from Mussolini, the Italian ally of Adolf Hitler during World War II, was quite clear. Trump had taken the statement from a Twitter account with the username @ilDuce2016. Benito Mussolini was known as Il Duce.

Trump's presidential campaign is thoroughly infused with racist ideology because Trump's strategy has been to use the legacy of popular racism in the United States to bring together a firm political base upon which to grow his candidacy. Adolf Hitler used a similar strategy in his own struggle to become the supreme leader of Germany.

Like the United States, Germany had a long legacy of pervasive racist ideology. Anti-Semitism was not the invention of the Nazis. Its practice went back at least as far in time as the Crusades, when Germanic armies preparing to fight against Muslims in the Middle East went on bloody rampages against Jewish communities all along the way, starting in the area now known as Germany.

Martin Luther, the German leader of the Protestant Reformation, wrote a text called On The Jews And Their Lies, in which he advised his Christian followers to "be on your guard against the Jews, knowing that wherever they have their synagogues, nothing is found but a den of devils in which sheer self-glory, conceit, lies, blasphemy, and defaming of God and men are practiced most maliciously and veheming his eyes on them."

Luther called upon his countrymen to begin a project of ethnic cleansing against the Jews. "Eject them forever from this country," he wrote. "For, as we have heard, God's anger with them is so intense that gentle mercy will only tend to make them worse and worse, while sharp mercy will reform them but little. Therefore, in any case, away with them!"

Luther was not content to merely encourage other Germans to persecute Jews. He personally led pogroms against them in several towns. Luther instructed the leaders of German cities to, "First to set fire to their synagogues or schools and to bury and cover with dirt whatever will not burn, so that no man will ever again see a stone or cinder of them. This is to be done in honor of our Lord and of Christendom, so that God might see that we are Christians, and do not condone or knowingly tolerate such public lying, cursing, and blaspheming of his Son and of his Christians... Second, I advise that their houses also be razed and destroyed. For they pursue in them the same aims as in their synagogues. Instead they might be lodged under a roof or in a barn, like the gypsies. This will bring home to them that they are not masters in our country, as they boast, but that they are living in exile and in captivity, as they incessantly wail and lament about us before God. Third, I advise that all their prayer books and Talmudic writings, in which such idolatry, lies, cursing and blasphemy are taught, be taken from them. Fourth, I advise that their rabbis be forbidden to teach henceforth on pain of loss of life and limb."

You get the idea. Luther goes on and on, describing the best way to persecute the Jews in extreme detail. One form of oppression Luther recommended that stands out in particular was the prohibition on Jewish travel between states. Luther's anti-Semitic travel ban and Donald Trump's proposed prohibition on Muslim travel are cut from the same cloth.

Just as Adolf Hitler's anti-Semitism arose out of a long history of discrimination, so has the racism of Donald Trump. The ugly American tradition of racial segregation for example, was echoed in Trump's early business career.

In 1973, the United States Department of Justice took the Trump Management Company, of which Trump was President, to court. The Trump Management Company was accused of apartment leasing discrimination against

African-Americans. Investigators had uncovered a pervasive practice in Trump's company of lying to African-American families, telling them that none of Trump's apartments were available for lease, when in fact, there were many ready to be rented. Trump's business was also accused of charging higher fees and insisting upon stricter leasing terms to African-American families than it provided to European-American families.

The case was settled out of court. As part of the settlement, Trump agreed that his company would not discriminate against African-Americans, and would share records of the apartments his company had available. The Trump Management Company just couldn't keep from discriminating against African-Americans, however, and in 1976, Trump's business was brought back into court for continuing to practice illegal racist segregation in housing.

Donald Trump was practicing Jim Crow in New York City. The city's human rights commission had to send investigators to report on Trump's racist leasing practices for years.

It wasn't the last time his racism was exposed in public. In 1989, Trump expressed envy at the remarkable advantages that he believed come from being African-American, saying, "If I was starting off today, I would love to be a well-educated black because I really do believe they have the actual advantage today."

Is Donald Trump right? Do young African-Americans really have an advantage over young European-Americans?

It's now 27 years after Trump made his remark, and it's often said that racism in America isn't as bad today as it used to be. Nonetheless,

- African-Americans have just 2.7 percent of the wealth in our country, even though they are 13 percent of the population
- African-American children are punished 300% more often than European-American children
- African-American juvenile offenders are put

on trial as adults more often than European-American juvenile offenders

- When African-Americans and European-Americans are sentenced for committing the very same crimes, African-Americans receive more severe punishments
- 37 percent of the people arrested for drug offenses are African-Americans, but African-Americans commit just 14 percent of drug offenses in the United States
- On average, African-Americans begin life in families with less money than European-Americans
- African-Americans are more likely to be searched when they are stopped for traffic violations than European-Americans are, and are stopped by police at a higher rate, even though they violate traffic laws at the same rate as European-Americans
- African-Americans are kept off of juries at a higher rate than European-Americans
- African-Americans with the same credit scores as European-Americans are more likely to have their mortgage applications rejected
- People with names that are judged to sound African-American are less likely to be asked for job interviews than people with names that seem European-American, even when their resumes are exactly the same
- African-Americans are more likely to go to poorly-funded schools than European-Americans

These aren't the kinds of advantages that anyone would want to deal with. The kind of advantages that Trump had, like a father with a vast financial fortune, powerful friends at the top of New York City government, a swanky private school education, and a well-paying job guaranteed straight out of college, are more along the lines of what most people would like to have.

Trump's long public record of conspicuous racism and recent plans for new, government-sponsored systems of discrimination on the basis of ethnicity, religion, sexual orientation and disability have excited the members of extremist nationalist groups. Before the 2016 Trump campaign appeared, the membership of these groups had been sagging. Now, they're ramping up for a new round of white supremacist militancy, seeing Trump as their hero.

During the campaign, the American Nationalist Super PAC paid to have explicitly racist pro-Trump robocalls made to likely Republican voters across the country, with messages such as "We don't need Muslims. We need smart, well-educated white people."

In Minnesota, the PAC sent out this message to voters over the telephone: "The American Nationalist Super PAC makes this call to support Donald Trump. I am William Johnson, a farmer and white nationalist. The white race is dying out in America and Europe because we are afraid to be called racist. This is our mind-set: It's OK that our government destroys our children's future, but don't call me racist. I'm afraid to be called racist. It's OK to give away our country for immigration, but don't call me racist. It's OK that few schools anymore have beautiful white children in the majority, but don't call me racist. Gradual genocide against the white race is OK, but don't call me racist. I'm afraid to be called racist. Donald Trump is not a racist, but Donald Trump is not afraid. Don't vote for a Cuban; vote for Donald Trump."

Trump's openly bigoted way of talking breaks with a tacit understanding within the Republican party that dates back half a century, to a time when many Democrats disaffected by their party's support for feminism and civil rights shifted their party loyalty to the GOP. Republicans embraced the agenda of these racist and sexist Democratic defectors, but there was an unspoken rule. It was no longer acceptable to speak openly of African Americans as inferior. People could still express racist or sexist ideas, but they had to do so in code, with ideas like demographic problems, urban crisis, the cycle of poverty, how feminism had gone too far, or the negative effects of affirmative action.

Trump simply ignores these implicit codes. He doesn't talk about problems with "immigration". He calls immigrants criminals and rapists. He doesn't say that Hillary Clinton was just defeated. Trump says that she was "schlonged." He has brought back a kind of straight talk about race and gender that is disturbing to many Americans, but has been sorely missed by others.

It's become nearly impossible to keep up with the barrage of bigotry coming from the Trump for President campaign, it comes out so rapidly. In this sense, Trump seems to be applying Adolf Hitler's observation about the power of overwhelming verbal assault: In Mein Kampf, Hitler wrote that, "At a given sign it unleashes a veritable barrage of lies and slanders against whatever adversary seems most dangerous, until the nerves of the attacked persons break down... This is a tactic based on accurate estimation of all human weaknesses, and its result will lead to success with almost mathematical certainty."

Hitler's faith in the power of overwhelming aggression was not restricted to mere verbal rhetoric, of course. He urged the use of extreme physical violence in order to force enemies into submission. "Terror cannot be overcome by the weapons of the mind but only by counter-terror," he wrote.

Donald Trump expressed the same idea when he told his supporters that, "The other thing with the terrorists is you have to take out their families, when you get these terrorists, you have to take out their families." It's a war crime to purposefully target civilians in order to intimidate one's enemy. Donald Trump doesn't care for such restrictions, but it's important to remember what provoked the creation of the current international system of laws of warfare in the first place.

The Geneva Conventions of 1949 were created in reaction to the atrocities of World War II, many of which were committed by the Nazis. Convention IV explicitly forbids the execution of civilians, even in time of war. In rejecting this standard, and advocating for the assassination of the families of alleged terrorists, Trump is seeking to take the world back to the horrors of the 1940s.

Among the horrors created by the Nazis were concentration camps, where millions of people were starved, tortured, worked to death, or simply murdered. For Adolf Hitler, these camps were part of "the final solution".

Although he has yet to imagine a scope of concentration camps that would come anywhere close to the scale of those built by the Nazis, Donald Trump is an advocate for brutal prison camps of his own sort. Trump's advocacy of brutal prison camps comes in reaction to the more liberal plans of the Obama Administration. In February 2016, Barack Obama declared that he would make a final effort to close the prison camps at the U.S. military base at Guantanamo Bay on the island of Cuba.

The Guantanamo Bay prison camps became infamous under George W. Bush, when it was revealed that prisoners there were subjected to repeated torture. Although the Bush Administration insisted that all of the people imprisoned in Guantanamo Bay were "the worst of the worst", for years there was no legal proceeding to determine whether there were any credible allegations against the prisoners at all. When military commissions finally were established as the sole legal proceedings available to prisoners in Guantanamo Bay, they shocked the world, seeming more like the kangaroo courts established by authoritarian regimes than anything else.

The accused were deprived of full and independent representation before the tribunals. Evidence obtained under torture would be permitted, and the accused would in many cases not even be allowed to know what evidence was being used against them.

Many of the Guantanamo Bay prisoners had been captured far away from any battlefield, and so could not credibly be assigned the legal status of prisoners of war. What's more, the Guantanamo Bay prisons did not meet the standards of the Geneva Conventions, which include legal standards for the imprisonment of soldiers during war time. Many of the prisoners turned out to have no connection to terrorism at all, while others were only tangentially connected to organizations that themselves had connections to terrorism, and weren't personally involved in the planning or execution of terrorism. Some of the prisoners were children.

Donald Trump responded to the news of the White House's determination to close the Guantanamo Bay prisons by telling his supporters, "This morning I watched President Obama talk about Gitmo, right, Guantanamo Bay - which, by the way we are keeping open, and we're going to load it up with some bad dudes, believe me. We're going to load it up."

Trump's ideas for what to do with large number of "bad dudes" he plans to load into prison camps such as Guantanamo were made plain when he told another audience a story about a mass murder of prisoners of war attributed to General John Pershing.

"Early in this century, last century, General Pershing, did you ever hear? Rough guy. Rough guy. They had a terrorism problem, and there's a whole thing with swine and animals and pigs, and you know the story. They don't like them, and they were having a tremendous problem with terrorism, and by the way, this is something you can read in the history books, not a lot of history books, because they don't like teaching this, and General Pershing was a rough guy, and he sits on his horse, straight like a ramrod, and it was early 1900s, and this was a terrible problem.

They were having terrorism problems, just like we do, and he caught fifty terrorists who did tremendous damage and killed many people, and he took the fifty terrorists, and he took fifty men, and he dipped fifty bullets in pig's blood. You heard that, right? He took fifty bullets, and he dipped them in pig's blood, and he had his men load his rifles and he lined up the fifty people, and they shot forty-nine of those people, and the fiftieth person, he said: 'You go back to your people and you tell them what happened.'... So we better start getting tough, and we better start getting vigilant, and we better start using our heads, or we're not going to have a country, folks! We're not going to have a country."

This story combines a certain glee in the idea of forcing Muslims to violate the dictates of their religion with a disregard for basic human rights. Muslim religious leaders were outraged at Trump's delivery of this story, but explained that the horror Muslims feel in its telling comes from its glory in killing, not in the detail of dipping bullets in pigs' blood.

It may be easy for Trump to imagine such a scenario when the only images he has seen of war have been Hollywood-produced fight scenes projected up onto a movie screen, but the plain fact is that the story Trump told about General Pershing is only a story. There is no evidence at all that any such event ever took place. It appears to be an urban legend, not actual history.

It's bad enough that Trump can't distinguish between fact and fiction. It's worse that the fictions Trump chooses to believe are sadistic.

It's a war crime to conduct mass executions of prisoners of war. Convention III of the Geneva

Conventions specifically prohibit the execution of prisoners of war without fair trial. The convention outlaws "the passing of sentences and the carrying out of executions without previous judgment pronounced by a regularly constituted court affording all the judicial guarantees which are recognized as indispensable by civilized peoples."

Three quarters of a century ago, the United States fought against Adolf Hitler so that atrocities such as mass executions would no longer take place. Donald Trump wants to bring these crimes against humanity back.

Trump's habit of celebrating cruelty and injustice, on the battlefield and in domestic life, leads Danielle Allen, a political theorist at Harvard University, to conclude that, "Donald Trump has no respect for the basic rights that are the foundation of constitutional democracy, nor for the requirements of decency necessary to sustain democratic citizenship. Nor can any democracy survive without an expectation that the people require reasonable arguments that bring the truth to light, and Trump has nothing but contempt for our intelligence."

Trump's strategy of political brutality seems to copy Hitler's skill at overwhelming his audience's capacity for reason with raw emotion, using the posture of fury as a political tool. Trump openly celebrates the power of anger.

Of the statements made by Trump during the 2016 election and checked by PolitiFact, 70% were found to be false or mostly false, and another 15 percent were found to be only half truths. That's far more than any other politician PolitiFact has ever checked. Hillary Clinton's statements were found to be false or mostly false 26% of the time, as a point of comparison.

Trump has lied about serious things, claiming that there were millions of votes illegally cast by undocumented immigrants in the 2016 presidential election – but there's no evidence for any such claim. Many of his lies are about relatively trivial things, like denying he played golf with

Samuel L. Jackson.

We live in an age when, with the Internet, checking simple facts is easier than has ever been before. So, every time Donald Trump has been caught in a lie, political commentators have predicted that his campaign would crumble as a result. These predictions have not borne fruit, but still the predictions of Trump's imminent demise keep coming. Many pundits now predict that Trump will be kicked out of office long before his four-year term in office is completed.

Trump's predicted self-destruction still hasn't taken place. To the surprise of many, repeated exposure of Trump's lies has had no impact on his popularity or credibility. He is still widely seen as straight-talking and genuine. A number of factors appear to contribute to this, revealing why the USA in 2016 was such fertile ground for the precipitous rise of a bigoted demagogue.

Trump has flipped his penchant for getting the facts wrong from a liability into an advantage. In Trump's strange political frame, ignorance and error burnish his image as an unscripted and unrehearsed leader. Trump dares us to defeat that frame. As he asked Bill O'Reilly, "Am I gonna check every statistic?"

The typical presidential candidate is expected to verify facts before proposing policies aimed at changing them, but Trump has defined himself as an exception to the typical candidate. He doesn't lie in the way people are used to being lied to by politicians. He doesn't wait for results from focus groups and opinion polls, consult with handlers, then decide what to say. He simply talks. If he gets facts wrong, this only affirms his authenticity.

Trump seems to have learned from the example of authoritarian leaders like Benito Mussolini and Adolf Hitler that getting the facts wrong matters much less getting the emotion right. Just as Mussolini and Hitler saw that anger was the emotion most helpful in summoning and maintaining popular support, Trump decided that

2016 was the year when Americans would embrace their anger.

Trump embodies the rage that he wants to see in the world. In the foreword to his most recent book, Trump warned that, "Some readers may be wondering why the picture we used on the cover of this book is so angry and so mean looking. I had some beautiful pictures taken in which I had a big smile on my face. I looked happy, I looked content, I looked like a very nice person, which in theory I am. My family loved those pictures and wanted me to use one of them. The photographer did a great job. But I decided it wasn't appropriate. In this book we're talking about Crippled America— that's a tough title. Unfortunately, there's very little that's nice about it."

The meme of a Crippled America justifies all sorts of abuse in Trump's nationalist ideology. Particularly troubling is the way that Trump encourages bigotry among America's children. The Nazis organized Hitler Youth organizations to indoctrinate young Germans in nationalist ideology. Today, Youth for Trump has formed on the social media site, spreading messages with hashtags such as #IslamIsTheProblem and #MuslimsGoHome.

Trump also shares the Nazi Party's affection for censorship as a tool for social control. He has urged the creation of new limits on freedom of speech, using protection from terrorism as an excuse. "We're losing a lot of people because of the Internet," Trump says. "We have to see Bill Gates and a lot of different people who really understand what's happening and maybe, in some ways, closing that Internet up in some ways."

Are we losing a lot of people because of the Internet? How many people are dead because of terrorists sending email through the Internet?

The reflex is to presume that terrorism is a serious problem, and that the threat of terrorism justifies the sacrifice of some constitutional rights. In politics, however, reflexes can be deceiving.

Think this through: Have you ever witnessed a terrorist attack? Do you know anyone who has been killed in a terrorist attack? Has there ever been a terrorist attack in your neighborhood?

For almost all Americans, the answers to these questions will be "no". The terrorist attacks of September 11, 2001 were dramatic and terrifying, but it turns out that they were not part of a larger trend. Terrorist attacks in the United States are actually extremely rare.

More Americans are killed by dogs than are killed by terrorists. No one is suggesting that we round up all the dogs and euthanize them, or put them into canine concentration camps.

So, why are so many Americans so eager to give up their constitutional rights in order to provide the feeling of protection from terrorism?

Adolf Hitler was an expert at conjuring the specters of enemies who were plotting the destruction of Germany. He convinced an entire nation to turn itself inside out in order to defend itself from Jews, who were actually just a small, peaceful, law-abiding minority.

How far will Donald Trump persuade Americans to go in order to protect themselves from a threat of terrorism so small that, in the last 20 years, only about 6 millionths of one percent of the U.S. population has fallen prey to it?

One destination Trump clearly plans to direct America toward in his pursuit of absolute security is financial bankruptcy. Trump is vague about many of his policies, but he has specific plans to imitate Hitler in one practical respect: He wants to dramatically increase military spending.

"I'm going to make our military so big, so powerful, so strong, that nobody, absolutely nobody is ever going to mess with us," says Trump. He says that the United States isn't "winning" enough because its military is too small.

Hitler made the same argument. He insisted that Germany would be saved only if it could rebuild a military stronger than any of its neighbors. In Mein Kampf, he complained, "Today our Left-wing politicians in particular are constantly insisting that their craven-hearted and obsequious foreign policy necessarily results from the disarmament of Germany, whereas the truth is that this is the policy of traitors. To all that kind of talk the answer ought to be: No, the contrary is the truth. Your action in delivering up the arms was dictated by your anti-national and criminal policy of abandoning the interests of the nation."

Of course, big military spending didn't lead Germany to security, to peace, or to prosperity. It led Germany into ruin and defeat.

The United States already has the largest and most powerful military in the world. America's military spending is larger than the military spending of all the other countries on Earth combined. Why do we need to make it even bigger?

Donald Trump doesn't just advocate for bigger spending on the military. He also proposes using the military more often. Trump is no isolationist. Instead, he shares Adolf Hitler's eagerness to send armies off to fight.

It's true that Trump has boasted about his supposed opposition to the 2003 military invasion of Iraq, citing it as evidence of his superior wisdom. However, it's important to note that Trump only ever expresses opposition in terms of the Iraq War in particular. Trump is no opponent to war in general.

Furthermore, in contradiction to his repeated claims, Trump didn't ever actually speak out in opposition to the invasion of Iraq until after the war was widely recognized as a disaster. Back in 2002, when Congress was debating whether to approve George W. Bush's plan for a rushed bombing and invasion of the country, Donald Trump got on a nationally broadcast radio show and declared that yes, he thought that the plan to go to war in Iraq was a good idea. It seems that Trump's claims of having opposed the

Iraq War, made during the 2016 campaign, were little more than a tactic to exploit Hillary Clinton's greatest weakness among Democratic voters – her support for the rushed invasion of Iraq.

The foreign policy that Trump advocates now is centered around intimidation and outright violence. Trump derides President Obama's renewed military attacks in Iraq, and expansion of American attacks into Syria, not as excessive force, but as not nearly aggressive enough. "Gentle bombing," Trump calls it, in comparison with what he would like to do.

"I've been saying bomb the oil for years," Trump says. "We're going to get rid of ISIS. We're going to get rid of them fast!"

Trump supporters are taking the cue. At a rally in Pensacola, Florida, a group of young girls wearing outfits with a gaudy American flag motif took to the stage before Trump himself appeared, to warm up the crowd. They sang praises for Trump's promises of more war in the near future.

The lyrics of their song: "Cowardice? Are you serious? Apologies for freedom, I can't handle this. When freedom rings, answer the call! On your feet! Stand up tall! Freedom's on our shoulders, USA. Enemies of freedom, face the music! Come on, boys, take them down! President Donald Trump knows how to make America great. Deal from strength or get crushed every time!"

That group of girls ended up filing a lawsuit against the Trump for President campaign, charging that Trump had broken its promises to compensate the girls for their performance. "I've asked and asked them for many months to make it right, and they haven't," said the father who manages the group.

Trump is gaining support for his plans for more war from more than just troupes of dancing girls, of course. Right wing religious leaders are echoing his drumbeat for more fighting as well. Baptist preacher Robert Jeffress, for example, gave a sermon to his followers declaring that, "Government is never called upon to forgive. Government is never called upon to turn the other cheek. The responsibility of government, according to the word of God, is to protect its citizens. And one way the government protects its citizens is by securing the borders... You may not agree with everything Donald Trump says, but Donald Trump was absolutely right when he said, 'It is time to start bombing the you-know-what out of ISIS.' That is a biblical response."

Many Christians will be shocked to see a preacher from their own religion promoting the blatant sadism of Donald Trump. It's worth remembering, though, that the Nazi Party in Germany received a great deal of support from Christian individuals and organizations there, even when some dissident churches were targeted for destruction.

Turning the other cheek is a quiet act that usually doesn't earn much attention. A louder voice from American Christianity demands the righteous punishment of the wicked. Such is the Christianity of Donald Trump.

In Trump's ideology, righteous punishment includes the infliction of pain for its own sake. Trump, like Hitler, believes in the power of torture.

America's previous Republican president, George W. Bush, personally ordered the torture of prisoners. That torture was illegal, and ineffective. It never resulted in the revelation of information that could prevent a terrorist attack.

However, at least when torture was conducted under George W. Bush, at least it was done with a sense of purpose. Bush Administration officials made the claim that the torture they had ordered was serving a larger need. Furthermore, the Bush Administration acknowledged in the abstract that torture was illegal, and played rhetorical games to claim that the special techniques American soldiers and intelligence agents applied against prisoners, designed to cause pain, terror and psychological suffering, were not torture. That doesn't make the years of torture by Bush and his aides morally justifiable, but it does suggest that, though they were misguided, Bush Administration officials were at least trying to do the right thing.

Donald Trump has removed all of those veils, and nakedly promises that, yes, the U.S. government will torture people, without any concerns about the law or moral qualms.

"Would I approve waterboarding? You bet your ass I would. In a heartbeat! I would approve more than that," Trump told the audience at a rally during his campaign. "Even if it doesn't work, they deserve it anyway!"

As Hitler did, Trump depicts vulnerability as a moral fault, and argues that the "winners" in society have the right to power. He writes, "America needs to start winning again. Nobody likes a loser and nobody likes to be bullied. Yet, here we stand today, the greatest superpower on Earth, and everyone is eating our lunch. That's not winning."

Trump wouldn't merely approve the use of torture. He wouldn't do it reluctantly. He would do it eagerly. Trump would agree to the torture of people in a heartbeat. Even if it "doesn't work", if there is no possible practical benefit to torture, Donald Trump would have it done.

How is that any different from the cruel fascination with pain cultivated by the Nazi Party?

Like Hitler, Trump isn't concerned with compassion. He wants to win, and will use whatever tactics he believes will enable him to win.

"I will do whatever it takes," says Trump. Whatever it takes could include many terrible things.

Winning is everything for Trump. As a consequence, he respects leaders who display strength more than he respects leaders who work for openness, tolerance, and freedom. In the abstract, respect for strong leaders might sound like a positive trait. In application, however, centralization of power in the hands of an unrivaled executive can lead to disaster. Yet, this is just what Donald Trump is aiming to achieve in taking the presidency for himself. David Harsanyi, editor at The Federalist, calls this totalitarian ideology "Trumpism – a philosophy based on the vagaries of one man".

In 1990, Trump was interviewed by Playboy magazine. That year, the old Soviet Union was finally opening up to the rest of the world. Some of the old republics were beginning a retreat back into dictatorship, but Russia was out of the grips of Stalinist Communism.

Trump approved of the ending of the Soviet Union, but he didn't approve of the weakening of the country's centralized leadership. Rather than seeing the spread of protests as a sign of strengthening political liberty, he perceived them as a sign that Mikhail Gorbachev wasn't an adequate leader. "Their system is a disaster. What you will see there soon is a revolution; the signs are all there with the demonstrations and picketing. Russia is out of control and the leadership knows it. That's my problem with Gorbachev. Not a firm enough hand," Trump told Playboy.

The consequences for the people of the Soviet Union would be dire, Trump warned. Political protest would inevitably lead to a violent revolution overthrowing Gorbachev, Trump warned, saying, "I predict he will be overthrown, because he has shown extraordinary weakness. Suddenly, for the first time ever, there are coal-miner strikes and brush fires everywhere- which will all ultimately lead to a violent revolution."

There was an attempted coup d'etat in the Soviet Union the year after Trump made this prediction. It wasn't a violent revolution led by angry workers, however. It wasn't an extension of street protests. It was a bloodless coup made by hardline Soviet leaders, strongmen of the sort that Trump said Gorbachev needed to become. They wanted to re-impose all of the authoritarian Soviet structures that Gorbachev had been working to dismantle.

They failed.

It was, in part, political protests in the streets of Moscow that ended the 1991 coup against Gorbachev. The strongmen ended up as, to use Trump's vocabulary, "the losers".

Mikhail Gorbachev did lose power, but he relinquished it peacefully, not at gunpoint. Gorbachev didn't give up power to an authoritarian determined to restore centralized power across the Soviet Union. He gave way to Boris Yeltsin, who became the first political leader of the new Russia.

Trump's prediction that freedom to protest would lead to violent revolution in the Soviet Union was wrong. Everyone makes incorrect predictions some of the time, of course. What's relevant for Americans' efforts to understand Trump in the long years until 2020 is the nature of the prediction that he chose to make back in 1990. When he interpreted Gorbachev's moves toward democracy as signs of weak leadership, Donald Trump revealed a belief that authoritarianism is the most effective style of government, and that strongmen make the best leaders.

This faith in antidemocratic authority was revealed by another comment made in the Playboy interview. Trump declared admiration for the Chinese government's bloody crackdown against student protesters in Tiananmen Square. Trump suggested that it had been a mistake to allow the protests to grow as large as they had, saying, "When the students poured into Tiananmen Square, the Chinese government almost blew it. Then they were vicious, they were horrible, but they put it down with strength. That shows you the power of strength."

Then, Trump made a comment that became a drumbeat in his presidential campaign: "Our country is right now perceived as weak… as being spit on by the rest of the world." This comment was made 26 years before Trump was inaugurated as President.

As Adolf Hitler discovered, when people feel humiliated and desperate, they are liable to offer their support to anyone who provides them with a path to confidence and security. This psychological lesson applies equally to Donald Trump as it does to his supporters.

Over the last couple of years, many of Donald Trump's personality flaws, deceits, and failures have been exposed to the world. Just as Americans in our time have share some subjective feelings with the Weimar Germans, Donald Trump could be thought of in the same way. He has withstood devastating attacks that would have destroyed any other politician, but emerged with a thoroughly ruined reputation.

Even though he emerged victorious on Election Day, he continues to be mocked in a way that no other President Elect ever has been. Even the abuse that was hurled at Barack Obama after his election, with its absurd racist conspiracy theories, didn't reach the level that has been directed at Trump. Whether the abuse is justified isn't relevant to this point: Trump is paying attention to the insults, he is infuriated with them, and he isn't responding well.

Between Election Day and Inauguration Day, victorious presidential candidates traditionally lay low and mend fences. They bask in the warmth of the support they have garnered from millions of people. Reflecting upon the struggle of the campaign behind them, they consult with opponents and allies alike and emerge cooler, calmer, and wiser.

That's not how Trump spent his transition period. From almost as soon as his victory was declared, Trump began throwing temper tantrums on Twitter, railing against his critics, often in all caps with exclamation marks. Even on New Year's Eve, when he could have easily issued a boilerplate message about hope and peace in the year to come, Trump couldn't resist the opportunity to denounce his opponents. "Happy New Year to all, including to my many enemies and those who have fought me and lost so badly they just don't know what to do," he wrote

Even after he has won the ultimate prize that our society still has to offer, Donald Trump still feels like a loser. He has discovered that even being President of the United States doesn't protect a person from being rudely mocked. He has spent his entire life up to this point trying to prove his worth by erecting monuments to himself and piling scorn upon others, and none of it seems to have earned him much in the way of true respect.

Even as President, Trump appears to continue to feel like a victim of a society that has never, and will never understand his true greatness. So it is that, just days before his inauguration, Trump asked Americans a rhetorical question that shows the depths of his delusions of persecution: "Are we living in Nazi Germany?"

It's ironic that this question came from the American politician who has been compared to Adolf Hitler more than any other American leader in the many decades since World War II. Trump's many threats have inspired a wave of fear Americans, many of whom are openly speculating that they may soon need to flee the country to escape persecution. Yet, even as he seizes the most powerful position any human being can ever hope to take, Trump himself feels that he is being persecuted.

It's a strange perception for the President of the United States to have, but then, Trump has led a strange life. He has spent his life so warmly wrapped in the insulation of extreme privilege that the simple presence of legal accountability and open criticism feels to him like a Holocaust.

When Trump asked, "Are we living in Nazi Germany?" he was responding to reports by intelligence officers suggesting that he has been compromised by a long campaign by Russian spies to recruit him as a useful fool, cultivate him as an informant, blackmail him, and then plant him in the position he now takes but is incapable of enjoying, in the Oval Office.

To Donald Trump, being a President under the law appears to be insufficient. Having lived his entire life with the expectation of entitlement to treatment of a level above what others can expect, he feels persecuted whenever he is reminded that, under the law, even as President, he is subject to the same restrictions as everyone else.

For the rest of us, an investigation of evidence of cooperation with Russian spies in an attack against the United States seems reasonable. For Trump, the investigation feels like an injustice worthy of the question, "Are we living in Nazi Germany?"

What causes many Americans to fear the Trump presidency is, while America's new Commander-In-Chief is outraged at the idea that he should be subject to the law, he feels no qualms at violating the basic rights of other Americans.

When Trump planned the mass surveillance, imprisonment, and compulsory registration of Muslims, along with the issuance of religious identification papers and travel restrictions for them, he didn't stop to consider, "Are we living in Nazi Germany?"

When Trump announced his plans for torture, mass execution, and assassination of children, he didn't ask himself, "Are we living in Nazi Germany?"

When Trump forwarded the messages of American Nazis to his followers, and when his followers began responding to him Nazi salutes, Nazi slogans, and Nazi swastikas, he didn't ask the question, "Are we living in Nazi Germany?"

Instead, Trump stood back with self-satisfaction, congratulating himself for making America great again.

CONCLUSION

"Only by understanding how those who seek the power try to influence us, and how we often actively participate in our own manipulation, can we finally understand the dangers we face if we leave rationality and skepticism behind and, instead, put our faith in a leader with charisma." – Laurence Rees

It's obvious that Donald Trump is not the same person as Adolf Hitler. As President of the United States Trump will not replicate the exact policies and practices of Hitler. Trump was born the year after Hitler killed himself. He's an American. Hitler was German. Trump was born with millions. Hitler was born dirt poor.

These distinctions aren't the point. People who compare Trump and Hitler aren't proposing that Trump will soon walk out before television cameras with a swastika arm band tied over his jacket. As Mark Twain noted, history does not repeat itself. It rhymes. As we compare Trump and Hitler, we are looking for rhymes.

The historical, biographical and social distinctions between Donald Trump and Adolf Hitler are stark. However, they are not complete. When people compare Trump to Hitler, they're trying to understand whether Donald Trump might be the sort of person who, when granted power, could engage in the level of brutality that Hitler unleashed upon the world.

So, when people ask Steve Ross, who studies the history of fascism at the University of Southern California, whether Donald Trump is a fascist, Ross's response is to say no, because fascism was something very specific in the political history of the 20th century. Donald Trump isn't a fascist. He isn't a Nazi. He's something else, a new kind of brutal authoritarian leader, with similarities to fascists, but with new, cruel tendencies of his own.

Ross notes, upon reflecting on the actions and words of Trump on the campaign trail, "We had the same thing happening in Germany in the 1920s with people being roughed up by the Brownshirts and they deserved it because they were Jews and Marxists and radicals and dissidents and gypsies. That was what Hitler was saying... I'm not saying Trump is Hitler, but the logic of condoning violence against those who oppose you -- you can imagine, a man who would condone it as a candidate -- what would he do as an official president?"

What will Donald Trump do as President?

It would be profoundly unwise for Americans to evaluate the people who present themselves as candidates for President only according to what they say they would do. Wise voters know that presidential candidates often make many promises on the campaign trail that they do not follow through with once they move into the White House.

We try to judge the character of presidential candidates by comparing them to previous political leaders. We seek out similarities between current candidates and political leaders in the past whose achievements we admire. We skeptically examine politicians for signs of dangerous tendencies by looking for echoes of the despots of the past.

Donald Trump is not Adolf Hitler. Donald Trump is, in some important ways, like Adolf Hitler.

Andrew O'Hehir explains, "Trump is something like Hitler, and that the type of authoritarian personality — or non-personality, in both these cases — who rises to the top when a democracy collapses conforms to a general pattern. As I see it, the parallels between Trump and Hitler are at once superficial — because they are different men, in sharply different historical contexts — and profound, because the underlying pattern is so similar and so disturbing."

It's not just liberals who are concerned about Donald

Trump's nationalist extremism. Weeks before the Republican primaries began, Max Boot, a senior member of the conservative Council on Foreign Relations, wrote, "Trump is a fascist. And that's not a term I use loosely or often. But he's earned it."

David Boaz of the libertarian Cato Institute cautions that, "Not since George Wallace has there been a presidential candidate who made racial and religious scapegoating so central to his campaign. Trump launched his campaign talking about Mexican rapists and has gone on to rant about mass deportation, bans on Muslim immigration, shutting down mosques, and building a wall around America. America is an exceptional nation in large part because we've aspired to rise above such prejudices and guarantee life, liberty, and the pursuit of happiness to everyone. Equally troubling is his idea of the presidency - his promise that he's the guy, the man on a white horse, who can ride into Washington, fire the stupid people, hire the best people, and fix everything. He doesn't talk about policy or working with Congress. He's effectively vowing to be an American Mussolini, concentrating power in the Trump White House and governing by fiat."

Gospel musician Kirk

Franklin writes, "To every pastor that stood next to Donald Trump last week, I hope you now see why we're losing respect as Christians in the world... While you were so busy wanting 'camera time,' you didn't 'take time' to examine his character... Banning Muslims does not reflect our country, or our Christ. I am very disappointed in people that say they believe what I believe compromise that for contaminated influence. I'm done."

Christine Todd Whitman, a Republican former governor of New Jersey, comments, "Frankly, if you go and look at your history and you read your history in the lead-up to the Second World War this is the kind of rhetoric that allowed Hitler to move forward, because you had people who were scared the economy was bad, they want someone to blame."

Thomas Sowell of the conservative Hoover Institution warns that, "No doubt much of the stampede of Republican voters toward Mr. Trump is based on their disgust with the Republican establishment. It is easy to understand why there would be pent-up resentments among Republican voters. But are elections held for the purpose of venting emotions? No national leader ever aroused more fervent emotions than Adolf Hitler did in the 1930s. Watch some old newsreels of German crowds delirious with joy at the sight of him."

Any single similarity between Adolf Hitler and Donald Trump is, in itself, insignificant. The identification by any particular political group of a Trump-Hitler parallel could be easily dismissed. What we're seeing in the comparisons between Trump and Hitler in the context of the Trump presidency, however, is something more than that. It's become a point of cultural convergence that transcends the typical divisions between conservative and liberal, because fear of Trump's authoritarian tendencies operates on an entirely different level.

Never have so many different comparisons between an American politician and Adolf Hitler been made. It isn't just Trump's policies that are being linked to Hitler's. His language, his manners, his mannerisms, his political tactics, his supporters' behavior, his biographical and social connections are being noted as well. American liberals, conservatives, moderates, historians, artists, Holocaust survivors, and foreign leaders are taking note of the similarities.

Yet, the comparisons come along with increasingly fervent demands that no political leader ever be compared to Adolf Hitler. Those who make these demands for silence recognize that when the memory of Hitler is brought into a political conversation, a profoundly unsettling shift takes place.

We cannot blame people for being disturbed when

Donald Trump is compared to Adolf Hitler. We can take a critical perspective, however, and try to evaluate the deeper source of their unease.

As unsettling as it is to consider the possibility that a democratically-elected politician could exploit our support, and use the power of our government in order to commit atrocities, it is the responsibility of citizens in a democracy to make such considerations – and this responsibility does not end with casting a vote on Election Day.

Despite Trump's claims that we are a ruined nation that must be made great again, the United States of America has remained throughout the 21st century the most powerful nation that has ever existed, with a military more deadly than any other in human history. The person who exerts executive authority over the USA must be subjected to the harshest scrutiny.

Instead of blaming those who take note of similarities between Donald Trump and Adolf Hitler for our discomfort, American citizens should face their feelings of unease. We should expand our skepticism rather than suppressing it, so that every presidential candidate, not just Donald Trump, is subjected to the Hitler Test.

As Donald Trump takes power, let's talk more about the atrocities committed by Adolf Hitler and the Nazis, and the other authoritarians of the past. Instead of turning away, and pretending that the Holocaust was some unique aberration, and that Hitler was an unexplainable manifestation of pure evil, let's rededicate ourselves to understanding how the Nazis rose to power and used it to such terrible ends. Let's look at the many other instances of popularly-supported atrocities too, so that we understand the symptoms of growing totalitarianism.

Most importantly, let's reject the temptation to imitate Adolf Hitler ourselves. Let's avoid the easy path of attributing all evil to a single scapegoat, and casting it out of our sight to gain an irrational feeling of protection from it.

We must not pretend that Donald Trump alone represents the only voice of violent nationalism in the United States. His growing power is merely a manifestation of a more pervasive hardening of American culture. Just as Hitler did not rise to power on his own, neither can Donald Trump abuse the power of the Oval Office without the passive consent of millions of Americans.

As we note the similarities between Donald Trump and Adolf Hitler, we must also cast a critical gaze at ourselves. How much, each one of us should ask, am I similar to a citizen of the Third Reich? In the candidate I support, in the speeches I applaud, how far along the path toward authoritarian nationalism have I gone? How much further am I willing to go? When, finally, will I take action to protect democracy?

Doubt, but don't despair. As you compare yourself to a person in the crowd at a rally in Nazi Germany, listening to Adolf Hitler speak, recognize the opportunity for resistance as well. Ask yourself: What am I willing to do to take a stand? What will I do now, so that when future generations ask what I did in the time of President Trump, I will have a response of which I can be proud?

Horace Bloom

AFTERWORD:
ON TRUMP AND REALITY

David Byrne has suggested a reason that Trump supporters are "so seemingly unaware of his lies and bullshit, and the ridiculousness of many of his positions and ideas." Social media tends to present a "point of view that you already agree with, since you only see what your 'friends' are sharing. We all do this to some extent - your friends share news with you and presumably many of your friends share your viewpoints. The algorithms built into those social networks are designed to reinforce this natural human tendency and expand upon it - if you like this, you'll like this. The networks reinforce your existing point of view in order to give you more of what you like, as that will make you happy and keep you on the network - and, in turn, more ads can be accurately targeted your way."

People who disagree with Trump tend to have networks of friends who disagree with Trump, and tend to follow sources that disagree with Trump. The information they receive through social media will have a strong tendency to be critical of Trump. Their initial exposure to a statement made by Trump is likely to be critical, or indicate that it has already been debunked. This tendency extends to news sources that are linked to by their friends and referenced in the sources they follow. For people who agree with Trump, it is precisely the opposite. The information they receive through social media will have a strong tendency to present Trump in a positive light. If a claim made by Trump has been debunked, they are much less likely to hear about it.

Daniel Patrick Moynihan famously remarked that "You are entitled to your opinion, but you are not entitled to your own facts." This is changing as social media develops the ability to target fact claims to people who are already predisposed to accept them. Beliefs are reinforced whether or not they are true, while evidence challenging those beliefs becomes increasingly less visible. Different views arise not just from different frames of interpretation, but from different sets of fact claims. It becomes harder and harder for people to understand how someone could possibly hold different beliefs.

This dynamic may be part of the reason that so many people enthusiastically support Trump, while so many remain completely bewildered at how anyone could possibly find him credible. It may also be a reason he is in danger of remaining underestimated until it is too late.

Assuming that Trump and his supporters are simply engaged in building beliefs based on fact claims may distract us from important aspects of his appeal. Drawing on Roland Barthes, Judd Legum has commented on a way that Trump, a member of the World Wrestling Entertainment (WWE) Hall of Fame, conducted his campaign. While the other candidates acted like boxers, Trump has been acting more like a professional wrestler.

Legum writes, "This public knows very well the distinction between wrestling and boxing; it knows that boxing is a Jansenist sport, based on a demonstration of excellence. One can bet on the outcome of a boxing-match: with wrestling, it would make no sense. A boxing-match is a story which is constructed before the eyes of the spectator; in wrestling, on the contrary, it is each moment which is intelligible, not the passage of time... The logical conclusion of the contest does not interest the wrestling-fan, while on the contrary a boxing-match always implies a science of the future. In other words, wrestling is a sum of spectacles, of which no single one is a function: each moment imposes the total knowledge of a passion which rises erect and alone, without ever extending to the crowning moment of a result."

Pundits accustomed to the traditional rules of a presidential campaign have been observing for a while now that Trump has lost the game as it is understood by its traditional rules. In July of 2015, the New York Post called him "toast" after he insulted John McCain for his capture in Vietnam.

Trump's insult was outrageous. It broke the rules-not just the rules presidential campaigns are supposed to play by, but basic principles of humanity and decency.

In a typical campaign, such a blatant violation of the rules would signal a loss, but Trump isn't mounting a typical campaign. In Trump's campaign, as in professional wrestling, being outrageous and breaking the rules is the way a player wins the contest. Professional wrestling is a kind of theater in which larger-than-life champions of good square off against exaggerated caricatures of evil. According to this code, the hero wins by transgressing the rules of a corrupt system.

"Some fights," Barthes observes, "among the most successful kind, are crowned by a final charivari, a sort of unrestrained fantasia where the rules, the laws of the genre, the referee's censuring and the limits of the ring are abolished, swept away by a triumphant disorder which overflows into the hall and carries off pell-mell wrestlers, seconds, referee and spectators."

As with the rigged rules of the game a wrestling hero rebels against, American politics is perceived by Trump's supporters as a corrupt system. Voting is presented as a way for citizens to exercise power, but this is increasingly viewed as an illusion concealing a corrupt reality that denies power to the average citizen. Party insiders, wealthy donors, super PACs, and other shadowy power brokers make the real decisions behind the scenes.

Trump's supporters see the electoral system as a kind of theater with a predetermined outcome. Their engagement with democracy, in this way, is not so different from watching a professional wrestling exhibition.

IS IT TOO LATE?

The future of a Trump presidency is a frightening prospect for many Americans. Even before Election Day 2016, the unprecedented aggression at the core of Donald Trump's political power had already been creating fundamental damage to American democracy for a year and a half.

Consider the example of Mercutio Southall, a protester who was attacked at a Trump rally in Birmingham, Alabama in the autumn of 2015.

Southall suffered a concussion, but the damage inflicted in the attack went beyond mere physical injury. His attack came not just at the hands of security, but also from members of the crowd. He was not just forcibly removed from the event. He was thrown to the ground, kicked, punched, choked, and called racist epithets including "monkey" and "nigger."

Trump's comment when asked about Southall was this: "Maybe he should have been roughed up." The attack against Southall was not the only time racial violence was perpetrated by Trump supporters during the 2016 presidential campaign season. Trump's comments afterwards were not the only time he sanctioned racist violence.

Racist mob violence does more than hurt bodies. It sends a message of degradation and intimidation to all members of the minority groups that come under attack. It emboldens people to make similar attacks in the future, while causing entire populations to live in fear.

Hitler's violence against racial minorities is remembered for its institutional efficiency. But before there was Auschwitz, there was Kristallnacht. The name given to the infamous evening of November 9, 1938 means "crystal night", referring to the shards of glass that came the smashed windows of Jewish homes, businesses, and synagogues across Germany. The destruction was perpetrated by citizens and brownshirts. Government officials looked on while the violence was taking place and allowed it to proceed.

Dozens were killed on Kristallnacht, but the damage went beyond that. The message was sent to ethnic and religious minorities that they could be harmed with impunity.

During his campaign, Trump promised that, if elected, he would create a "deportation force" to round up and expel eleven million undocumented immigrants from the United States within a period of two years. Faced with daunting obstacles after his election, Trump scaled back this threat to a forced expulsion of three million undocumented immigrants, but pledged that the expulsion would begin immediately after his inauguration.

Though scaled down, this forced expulsion would be still comparable in scale to the one carried out by Hitler in his early years. It would require the creation of an extensive system of detention facilities and a huge police force whose sweeping raids would devastate families and communities throughout the United States. Outside the United States, it would create a massive humanitarian crisis with the flood of millions of deportees into refugee camps in Mexico and other Latin American nations.

The very proposal has already led to widespread insecurity and fear. Mycee Pineda, an undocumented immigrant from the Philippines, a former colony of the United States, has been working and paying taxes in America for years. Now, she worries that her contributions will be ignored, and she will be seized by Trump's deportation troopers. "What will happen to an immigrant like me who has been active in my community, paying my taxes, and taking care of my parents?", she wonders. "Will I be deported?"

Among Trump's supporters, the desire to shut down dissenting voices goes beyond denigrating and bypassing the press. Washington State Senator Doug Ericksen has proposed legislation that would define any protest that causes economic disruption as "economic terrorism."

ACLU spokesman Doug Honig has noted that under Ericksen's proposed law, even peaceful protests like the lunch counter sit-ins of the civil rights movement would be considered a form of terrorism. This is a stark departure from the way nonviolent civil disobedience has been understood in the context of American society. According to this view, historical figures including Susan B. Anthony, Martin Luther King, and Henry David Thoreau would be re-defined as terrorists. Anti-war efforts throughout American history, the women's suffrage movement, and the civil rights struggle would be denigrated as terrorist activities. This perspective threatens to erase the understanding of America as a country that has benefited from changes brought about in response to peaceful resistance.

Tremendous harm has already been caused by Trump's repeated sanction of racist mob violence, insults against religious and ethnic minorities, promises of torture, and threats of the detention and deportation of millions. Externally, international trust in the stability of the United States has been shaken. Internally, huge numbers of people – citizen and immigrant alike - no longer feel safe within the American borders.

Milwaukee County Sheriff David Clarke, who Trump reportedly considered for head of Homeland Security, has also called for a greatly expanded crackdown on terrorism. He has called for anyone "spewing jihadi rhetoric" to be questioned without an attorney, deprived of habeas corpus, and detained indefinitely at Guantanamo Bay. He estimates the number of people that would be imprisoned this way to be in the hundreds of thousands, perhaps up to a million.

Trump himself has proposed revocation of citizenship as a punishment for burning the flag. This may have been intended as a display of patriotism, but in reality it is the opposite. It would undermine well-established understandings of the rights of Americans, and establish an extreme penalty for constitutionally protected expression.

Trump's threat to revoke citizenship as punishment for the non-violent expression of dissent is especially alarming in light of his proposal to create a deportation force large enough to sweep up, detain and deport eleven million people over the course of two years. Removal of citizenship for political dissenters would potentially put them under this massive system of detention, along with people of disfavored religions or national origins. If enacted, this would be disturbingly similar to the pattern of detentions that occurred under Hitler.

Many question whether it is too late to turn aside the growth of Trumpist nationalism. All three branches of the federal government will soon be under Donald Trump's control. Although some among the leadership of the Republican Party made a show of defiance in 2016, after the election, they have surrendered, and have made it plain that they will do nothing significant to stand in the way of Trump's agenda.

Even Mitt Romney, the 2012 Republican presidential nominee who in March of 2016 warned that, "If we Republicans choose Donald Trump as our nominee, the prospects for a safe and prosperous future are greatly diminished," visited Trump after the election and humbled himself, begging to be allowed to serve as a loyal member of Trump cabinet before Trump gleefully turned him away.

"Donald Trump lacks the temperament to be President," Romney once said. "Dishonesty is Donald Trump's hallmark." However, although Romney once declared, "Mr. Trump is a con man, a fake," Romney and his establishment Republican followers now seem to want to join in the con. Americans can no longer count on them to stand in the way of Trump's dangerous totalitarian impulses.

However, many of the institutional safeguards of American democracy remains. Mercutio Southall and another Black Lives Matter protester who was violently ejected from the trump rally along with him have filed a lawsuit against Donald Trump in federal court. Southall's suit faces difficult odds, but still could succeed in holding Trump accountable for the consequences of his demagoguery. "Trump's intentional acts of inciting violence cannot be allowed from anyone," the lawsuit states, serving as a rallying point for those who assert that even a billionaire President is not above the law.

Another institutional safeguard is the free press. One of Donald Trump's more alarming similarities to Adolf Hitler is his use of the phrase "lying press", a literal translation of the Nazi term "lügenpresse". Jeff Nesbit, a former communications director for Vice President Dan Quayle warns that "Lügenpresse has traveled across the ocean to Trump rallies and social media posts from Trump's legion of alt right supporters."

As the Trump for President campaign lurched toward Election Day, its leader's fury at journalists increased, until he began to whip crowds of his supporters up into such an anti-reporter frenzy that journalists covering his rallies could only leave under the protection of security guards. Tommy Burr, President of the National Press Club, issued a statement of special concern just a few weeks before the end of the campaign, saying, "We find this renewed pattern of journalist intimidation to be unacceptable and dangerous to our democracy."

Former Secretary of Labor Robert Reich has identified seven methods used by tyrants to erode the freedom and independence of the press, all of which are employed by Donald Trump. These methods include berating, threatening, blacklisting, limiting access, turning the public against the media, and bypassing the media altogether to address the public directly. "Responsible media," observes

Reich, "hold the powerful accountable by asking them hard questions and reporting on what they do. Apparently Trump wants to eliminate such intermediaries."

Trump has threatened to censor journalists whose opinions he doesn't like. He has kicked reporters out of press conferences when they dare to ask challenging questions. He has attempted to replace access for journalists with a Twitter account. It is essential for Americans to recognize the difference, and to do their part to sustain vigorously independent journalism that is willing to defy Trump's glowering intimidation.

It isn't enough just for journalists to speak out, of course, The right of people to disagree and to protest is an essential element of a free and democratic society. It is an important factor in preventing us from descending into tyranny. The First Amendment guarantees the "right of the people peaceably to assemble, and to petition the Government for a redress of grievances," yet it is precisely this right that Trump and his supporters are attacking. Since winning the election, Trump and a number of his supporters have put forward a vision of an America in which civil space is dramatically reduced, and non-violent dissent is harshly punished.

Trump's allies in Congress have voted to prohibit members from protests on the House floor. America's best legislators are continuing their dissent nonetheless. Trump's transition team shut off huge areas of Washington DC for the inauguration in order to prevent peaceful protest. Huge swarms of protesters came to DC anyway.

Americans still have time to limit the harm caused by the Trump White House and its supporters, if they accept that the threat has become serious, and is no longer something to simply laugh at and and quickly dismiss, like the crude antics of a reality TV show clown being intentionally provocative for the cameras.

Horace Bloom

OTHERS' STATEMENTS ON TRUMP

Peter Ross Range, author of 1924: The Year that Made Hitler:

"To any serious student of Hitler's frightening and unforeseen rise to power in Germany, the recurring echoes in Trump's speeches, interviews and his underlying thinking have become too blatant to overlook."

Harry Rosenfeld, Editor of the Albany Times-Union and refugee from Nazi Germany:

"There are many reasons for this year standing out, widely expostulated by the news media. Yet all the column inches of exemplary enterprise journalism only glancingly touched on what I consider most threatening to our country. And that is the striking congruities between the traits and techniques displayed by Trump in his climb to power and those manifested by Adolf Hitler when he battled for his nation's leadership in the early 1930s."

Statement from the American Civil Liberties Union:

"Donald Trump's proposal to bar Muslims from entering our country based solely on their faith is blatantly unlawful and fundamentally un-American. We are a nation of immigrants, many of whom came to this country to escape prejudice and discrimination. We urge all of our political leaders to categorically reject this dangerous escalation of hateful rhetoric because it undermines our core American values."

Martin O'Malley, former Democratic presidential candidate:

"Now is not the time for reconciliation. Dietrich Bonhoeffer didn't reconcile with the Nazis. MLK didn't reconcile with the KKK. Now we fight."

Letter to Donald Trump from the Muslim Public Affairs Council:

"Ever since you announced your run for Presidency of the United States, you have scapegoated the American Muslim community and other minority groups for all your perceived ills of America.

The truth is that you – and your supporters -- are scared of anything that is different than you.

You rely on the promotion of fear and Internet lies to fuel the flames of hate and divisiveness across our country.

You have no understanding of the world in which you live. That's why you insist on backward policies, such as building walls and segregating communities based on religion, as a desperate attempt to create a false sense of strength and security, and to preserve your distorted view of what makes America great.

Well, we have news for you: We will no longer be bullied. We will no longer be your punching bag.

We challenge you to a debate with a representative from the American Muslim community on the issues you have raised about Islam and Muslims.

We are confident that you, a person of great rhetorical ability, will appreciate this opportunity to showcase to America your strength and knowledge in such matters."

Kirk Douglas:

"I've also lived through the horrors of a Great Depression and two World Wars, the second of which was started by a man who promised that he would restore his country it to its former greatness. I was 16 when that man came to power in 1933. For almost a decade before his rise he was laughed at, not taken seriously. He was seen as a buffoon who couldn't possibly deceive an educated, civilized population with his nationalistic, hateful rhetoric. The 'experts' dismissed him as a joke. They were wrong... Until now, I believed I had finally seen everything under the sun. But this was the kind of fear-mongering I have never before witnessed from a major U.S. presidential candidate in my lifetime."

Statement by Council on American-Islamic Relations Chair Nihad Awad:

"Donald Trump's inflammatory rhetoric has crossed the line from spreading hatred to inciting violence. By directly stating that the only way to stop terrorism is to murder Muslims in graphic and religiously-offensive ways, he places the millions of innocent, law-abiding citizens in the American Muslim community at risk from rogue vigilantes. He further implies that our nation should adopt a strategy of systematized violence in its engagement with the global Muslim community, a chilling message from a potential leader. We pray that no one who hears this message follows his gospel of hate."

From A Letter to Donald Trump from Amara Majeed:

With all due respect, Mr. Trump, you are a demagogue who is capitalizing on Americans' fear and paranoia; you are scapegoating an entire population of 1.6 billion people in an attempt to further your campaign, in an attempt to "make America great again." But the effect of this is that by advocating for the registration of Muslim Americans and the banning of Muslims from entering the United States, you are providing a platform on which the marginalization of and discrimination against an entire group of people becomes justifiable, even "American." I could go on about how problematic it is that you equate the actions of a small extremist group with nearly a fourth of the world's population, but I find it to be of even greater interest that white supremacists are actually greater perpetrators of domestic terrorism compared to Muslim terrorists... You are dragging the American people back into the past, keeping us from moving forward. I have always believed that the rent I pay for being privileged enough to grow up in the United States is to contribute to the advancement of modern American society. And that's the thing, Mr. Trump: You can never take that away from me."

Statement from Mitt Romney – before the election:

"Mr. Trump is directing our anger for less than noble purposes. He creates scapegoats of Muslims and Mexican immigrants. He calls for the use of torture. He calls for killing the innocent children and family members of terrorists. He cheers assaults on protesters. He applauds the prospect of twisting the Constitution to limit First Amendment freedom of the press. This is the very brand of anger that has led other nations into the abyss. Here's what I know. Donald Trump is a phony, a fraud."

Psychiatrist and Holocaust Survivor Franz Wasserman:

"What we see now in our country is very similar to the early days of the Nazi rule in Germany: The Neo-Nazis and the KKK have become more prominent and get recognition in the press. We are all familiar with Trump's remarks against all Muslims and all Mexicans. But there has not been anything as alarming as the appointment of Steve Bannon as Trump's chief strategist. Bannon has, apparently, made anti-Semitic remarks for years, has recently condemned Muslims and Jews, and he and Lt.

Gen. Michael Flynn, the pick as national security advisor, advocate the political and cultural superiority of the white race. At the same time Trump is trying to control the press. Thus the entire Nazi ideology is in place already in and around the new government. How far will it get?"

From the Anti-Defamation League:

"Donald Trump's hate speech against immigrants is highly inappropriate and we join with the voices of many others around the country who have condemned his offensive remarks. It is time for Trump to stop spreading misinformation and hatred against immigrants, legal and undocumented."

Sabine Heinlein:

"I am beyond frustrated that we're stuck with a president who, just like Adolf Hitler, despises refugees, intellectuals, journalists, women and non-Christians. I am married to a Mexican immigrant, and both my husband and I became American citizens in order to be able to vote and perform jury duty."

Political Theorist Danielle Allen:

"Like any number of us raised in the late 20th century, I have spent my life perplexed about exactly how Hitler could have come to power in Germany. Watching Donald Trump's rise, I now understand."

From the United Kingdom's Prime Minister David Cameron:

"I think if he came to visit our country he'd unite us all against him."

From the Human Rights Campaign:

"Donald Trump has pandered his way to the top of the field by opposing the most basic protections for LGBT people and supporting Kim Davis-style discrimination against LGBT people," said Human Rights Campaign President Chad Griffin. "What's more, despite being married three times himself, this is a candidate who says he looks forward to appointing justices who would overturn marriage equality for loving same-sex couples. Donald Trump's calculated efforts to use division, fear and bigotry to score political points is as dangerous as it is vile."

Documentarian Ken Burns on Trump:

"He's set himself up to continue to roil that dark unconscious that he has tapped into for his base. The fat that he could say the things he said about women, and that his adoring masses are not even flinching about that, is Hitler-esque."

From Zeev Hod, Holocaust Survivor and History Teacher:

"If anyone dared to heckle Hitler, the S.A. would beat them to a pulp. They were essentially thugs. Not that different from what we see at Trump's rallies today."

Shakira:

"This is a hateful and racist speech that attempts to divide a country that for years has promoted diversity and democracy. No one living in this century should stand behind so much ignorance."

Bob Burnett:

"Both men had a penchant for telling outright lies. Hitler blamed the 1933 Reichstag fire on communists even though a single deranged man, Marinus van der Lubbe, was caught at the scene. After the December, 2015, San Bernardino shootings, Trump blamed the killings on Muslims, in general, and called for shutting down entry of Muslims into the United States as well as starting a registry of American Muslims."

J.K. Rowling on Trump:

"Voldemort was nowhere near as bad."

Praise for Donald Trump from retired Ku Klux Klan Grand Wizard David Duke:

"The Jewish knives are coming out on Donald Trump. How come it's against America values to want to preserve the heritage of the country? We're overwhelmingly a Christian country and overwhelmingly a European country."

"Make no mistake about it, our people played a huge role in electing Trump!"

"I represent the ideas of preserving this country and the heritage of this country, and I think Trump represents that as well."

The Crusader, the Official Newspaper of the Ku Klux Klan:

"'Make America Great Again' is a catchy slogan and we are beginning to see it and hear it everywhere. But can it happen? Can America really be great again? This is what we will soon find out! While Trump wants to make America great again, we have to ask ourselves, 'What made

America great in the first place?' The short answer to that is simple: America was great not because of what our forefathers did – but because of who our forefathers were. America was founded as a White Christian Republic."

BIBLIOGRAPHY

Armstrong, K. (2001). Holy war: The Crusades and their impact on today's world. New York: Anchor Books.

Ayçoberry, P. (1999). The social history of the Third Reich: 1933-1945. New York: New Press.

Blair, G. (2000). The Trumps: Three generations that built an empire. New York: Simon & Schuster.

Flood, C. B. (1989). Hitler, the path to power. Boston: Houghton Mifflin.

Gonen, J. Y. (2000). The roots of Nazi psychology: Hitler's utopian barbarism. Lexington, KY: University Press of Kentucky.

Hitler, A., & Murphy, J. V. (2011). Mein Kampf: The official 1939 edition. Arden, Warwickshire: Coda Books.

Johnson, E. A., & Reuband, K. (2005). What we knew: Terror, mass murder and everyday life in Nazi Germany: An oral history. Cambridge, MA: Basic Books.

Kaufman, M. T. (2003). Soros: The life and times of a Messianic billionaire. New York: Vintage Books.

Langer, W. C. (1943). A psychological analysis of Adolf Hitler. USA: Office of Strategic Services.

Noakes, J., & Pridham, G. (1975). Documents on Nazism, 1919-1945. New York: Viking Press.

Rees, L. (2012). Hitler's charisma: Leading millions into the abyss. New York: Pantheon Books.

Shirer, W. L. (1960). The rise and fall of the Third Reich; a history of Nazi Germany. New York: Simon and Schuster.

Steele, C. (2016). US presidential election: Republican candidate Donald Trump's activities in Russia and compromising relationship with the Kremlin.

Trump, D., & McIver, M. (2004). Trump: How to get rich. New York: Ballantine Books.

Trump, D. (2011). Time to get tough: Making America great again! Washington, DC: Regnery Publishing.

Trump, D. (2015). Crippled America: How to Make America Great Again. New York: Threshold Editions.

Trump, D. (2015). Donald Trump: Make America Great Again. Capitol Publishing.

Photo by Gage Skidmore

Photo by Heinrich Hoffmann, in the public domain

ABOUT THE AUTHOR

Horace Bloom is an electrical engineer, history buff, and amateur alpaca farmer living outside Eugene, Oregon. He is registered to vote as neither a Democrat nor a Republican, has much less than a billion dollars in assets, and has no ambition either to become a painter or to be elected to public office.